FINNISH MAGIC

Tap into a Rich Tradition

Since ancient times, the Finns have been noted for their magical traditions. The Danes believed that the Finns could control the wind. The English considered it bad luck to kill a Finn. In America, the Finns were targeted as witches.

The Finns were one of the last groups in Europe to be Christianized. The national epic of the Finns, the Kalevala, is a story of magic. That could be why they still practice the traditions of ancient shamans today.

Finnish Magic is the first book to focus on the magical traditions of the Finns. Explore techniques and practices passed down through the generations from shaman to shaman. Learn of the Finnish gods, spirits, and the rituals that the ancient mages used to gain power and knowledge. Discover one of the few European shamanic traditions that's still alive today and glimpse a whole new world of magic.

About the Author
Robert Nelson is a mental health counselor in Vancouver, Washington. He has a master's degree in Counseling and a doctorate in Psychology, and a degree in Asian Studies with a particular emphasis on comparative religion. He has conducted field studies on shamanism and comparative religion in Korea, Okinawa, and the Philippines. His published writings include articles on early American witchcraft, mental health counseling, military chaplains, and suicide prevention.

Dr. Nelson is a descendant of several witches mentioned in the witch trials of Salem and of the Finnish witch Margaret Matson, who was tried by William Penn. His interest in magic and the supernatural began with personal experiences as a child and have grown to include palmistry, scrying, Kabbalah, and ritual magic.

To Write to the Author
If you wish to contact the author or would like more information about this book, please write to the author in care of Llewellyn Worldwide and we will forward your request. Both the author and the publisher appreciate hearing from you and learning of your enjoyment of this book and how it has helped you. Llewellyn Worldwide cannot guarantee that every letter written to the author can be answered, but all will be forwarded. Please write to:

Robert Nelson
℅ Llewellyn Worldwide
P.O. Box 64383, Dept. K489-8
St. Paul, MN 55164-0383, U.S.A.

Please enclose a self-addressed, stamped envelope for reply, or $1.00 to cover costs. If outside U.S.A., enclose international postal reply coupon.

FINNISH MAGIC

A NATION OF WIZARDS
A WORLD OF SPIRITS

ROBERT NELSON, Ph.D.

1999
Llewellyn Publication
St. Paul, Minnesota 55164-0383

Finnish Magic: A Nation of Wizards, A World of Spirits ©1999 by Robert Nelson. All rights reserved. No part of this book may be used or reproduced in any manner whatsoever without permission from Llewellyn Publications except in the case of brief quotations embodied in critical articles and reviews.

First Edition
FIRST PRINTING, 1999

Cover design by Anne Marie Garrison
Cover illustration by Moon Deer
Editing and interior design by Astrid Sandell
Interior illustrations by Anne Marie Garrison

Library of Congress Cataloging-in-Publication Data
Nelson, Robert E., 1952–
  Finnish magic : a nation of wizards, a world of
spirits / Robert Nelson, Jr. -- 1st ed.
     p.   cm.
  Includes bibliographical references (p.).
  ISBN 1-56718-489-8
  1. Magic—Finland. 2. Witchcraft—Finland.
3. Kalevala. 4. Mythology, Norse. 5. Finns—United
States—History. I. Title.
BF1584.F5N44 1999
133.4'3'094897—dc21   98-31527
                                                          CIP

Publisher's Note: Llewellyn Worldwide does not participate in, endorse, or have any authority or responsibility concerning private business transactions between our authors and the public. All mail addressed to the author is forwarded but the publisher cannot, unless specifically instructed by the author, give out an address or phone number.

Printed in the United States of America

Llewellyn Publications
A Division of Llewellyn Worldwide, Ltd.
P.O. Box 64383, Dept. K489-8, St. Paul, MN 55164-0383

Llewellyn's World of Magic and Religion Series

At the core of every religion, at the foundation of every culture, there is magic.

Magic sees the world as alive, as the home which humanity shares with beings and powers both visible and invisible. You can interact with these powers to your advantage or disadvantage—depending upon your awareness and intention.

When you explore the magical system in this book, you will learn about these powers and how to connect with them using the centuries-old wisdom of the Finnish shamans.

Finnish magic grew from a shamanic tradition related to that of the North American Indian and the Inuit. Studying this ancient tradition will enhance your understanding of yourself and your connection with the universe—and it will link you with the forces and energies that permeate the world you live in.

DEDICATION

For those who know
and those who've known
whispered secrets late at night
laughter at unspoken punchlines
and the real meaning
of inspiration.

Table of Contents

Preface   *xiii*

A Nation of Wizards   1

The Kalevala: An Epic of Magic   25

The World of Spirits   43

Trance Work and Ritual   63

The Magic of Nature   77

The Magic of Song   93

The Sauna   111

Sacred Times   119

Dancing   133

The Symbols of Magic   139

Conclusion   *157*

Appendix: Finnish Language   *159*

Bibliography   *161*

Index   *165*

Preface

Trickster mountain played with me
Showed me visions
Played jokes on me
Changed rocks to rabbits
Unveiled the life inside her
Pulled me down close
To kiss her rock face

Crow flew close above me laughing
as I struggled to hold on
to my little reality

Trembling I try to fight the vision
Try to deny the spirit message
But hear still the white laughter
of the goddess

A prominent characteristic of Finnish magic is awareness. We do not need to create the numinous. Regardless of how we perceive it or what we call it—sacred, spiritual, divine, supernatural—it is real. By being open to experience and perceptions that are outside the boundaries of routine existence, we expand our capacity to enjoy. By increasing our awareness, we invite the sacred into our lives.

Recently, while climbing down from the summit of one of the Cascade volcanoes, I experienced a spontaneous sacred experience. Climbing down a talus ridge, I began to see strange things. I saw a rabbit sitting upright and still. He didn't move as I approached, then with only a foot or two between us, he changed into a rock. I began to see animals and animal parts. I could see individual hairs and variations in color and shadow. Then they would change—sometimes suddenly, sometimes gradually—into volcanic rocks.

I stepped carefully from rock to rock. Taking my time, I cautiously tested each rock. At one point the rock steps seemed solid, but then they seemed to move. I was thrown head first onto the talus. I was bruised on my knee and my torso, but there was no serious injury. Then there were more animals and a second fall. Although not seriously injured, I was shaking and had the feeling that the mountain had purposely thrown me down.

At first, I thought the mountain might be mad at me. I searched my mind for some uncleanness or irreverence. I spoke to the spirit of the mountain, an apology for any offense I might have given. Then I thought that perhaps the mountain just didn't like me.

The visual tricks continued. A junk car, a satellite disk, more animals—all transformed to rocks and boulders. On the ridge, on the glacier, and even on the wooded trail below, the tricks continued. I saw a sign posted on a tree. I could even make out writing on the sign, but as I approached it became just a lighter area of bark. An old water pump, junk, metal cords—these and other things became rocks, trees, and plants.

I began to suspect everything I saw. I suspected all my perceptions. Even in the car, the tricks continued. A man at the side of the road looked at me with dark eyes and smiled before transforming into a small tree. I was so suspicious that I watched two calves for several minutes, waiting for them to change, but they never did. The tricks or visions continued until I left the wilderness area.

Some might discount such experiences as psychic trash or elementals. They might view them as interesting but not significant. Others might discount them as hallucinations—the result of fatigue or altitude sickness.

Certainly such experiences can result from extreme stress. From ancient times, people have used physical stress to precipitate mystical states. Sweat lodges, long-distance running, vision quests, and even mountain climbing have been used to elicit such experiences. Others have used meditation, breathing exercises, isolation, and sensory deprivation. Even more "traditional" approaches rely on such techniques as fasting, rhythmic music, and austerities. The physiological connection doesn't invalidate the spiritual experience.

For those who are aware, the sacred is ever present. The mountain played with me. Just as an older brother sometimes plays too rough with a younger brother, so the mountain played with me. It was affection, not anger, I received that day. It was not Yahweh speaking to Moses on Mt. Sinai. It was not Sengen speaking with Jikigyo

Miroku on Mt. Fiji. It was the intelligent personality of a Cascade volcano playing with a friend. Perhaps not a major revelation, but definitely sacred. It would be no more reasonable to discount this contact with the mountain spirit than it would be to ignore beauty, intelligence, or grace regardless of the source.

The sacred is sacred whether small or large, human or natural, simple or profound. It is my prayer that this book will help us all to become more aware of the sacredness in our lives.

Ei lakia tarvita kun sovinnossa eletäën.
(You don't need laws when you live in harmony.)

Robert Nelson
Cascadia, Turtle Island
1998

A Nation of Wizards

A hardy solitary race dwells on the northern edge of the world. Their origins are lost somewhere in the shadows of pre-history. They speak a language that is more akin to Ugrian, Samoyed, and Korean than to the nearby Russian, German, or Swedish. In former days, their skill as woodsmen and warriors was rivaled only by their reputation as sorcerers. In modern times, they have become respected for the courageous defense of their homeland against overwhelming odds. These are the children of Kalevala—The Finns.

Origin of the Finns

The Finns came out of Asia thousands of years ago, but little is known of that time beyond history except for hints gleaned from archaeology and folklore. The Finns shared with their cousins, the Lapps, a belief in animism—that spirits reside in all things. And like other Asiatic people, they had shamans who, through communication with the spirits, could gain access to power used for healing or other purposes. Along with other people of the northern forests, the Finns had the bear cult, and as time went on they added Norse beliefs to their own. The Finns' oral tradition reaches back to the Stone Age, and includes stories of the gods and culture-heroes, as well as the magical lore of healing and communication with the gods.

The Finnic people are comprised of two major groups: the Volga-Finns (Maris or Cheremis and Mordvins) and the Balto-Finns (Estonians, Livonians, and Votes in the southern group and Vespians, Karelians, Izhorians, and Finns in the northern group). Finnish speakers probably arrived in their current homelands as early as 4,000 years ago, and it appears that earlier Finnic people lived farther south than modern Estonia. The Roman historian Tacitus mentioned several Finnic peoples, including the Aestii, ancestors of the modern Estonians. Aestii was the most common name for the Finnic people in the ancient times, both among themselves and to Germanic speakers. To the Scandinavians they were Sembi, and to the Slavs they were Pruzi (Prussians).

There is evidence that the Finno-Ugrians anciently occupied a major part of the Scandinavian Peninsula, and possibly part of the British Isles. J. F. Campbell and others have taught that the aboriginal inhabitants of the British Isles were Finns displaced by the conquering Celts and Germans, who seemed to associate the Finns with magic. The old Norse word for sorcery, *finngerd*, literally meant "a Finn's work."

Many Celtic myths reflect ideas of an older race. The Irish hero Cuchulinn may have originated from a Finno-Ugrian demigod. There are additional parallels between the Kalevala and the Irish legends. The Fomorians, who were submarine fairies in Irish legend, were in fact Finnish pirates. Finntan, the Irish Noah, had obvious Finnish characteristics reminiscent of Väinämöinen. Those interested in a more thorough study of prehistoric Finnish influence on the Celts will be interested in *The Druid Source Book From Earliest Times To The Present Day* (Blandford Press: London, 1996) edited and compiled by John Matthews.

Tacitus may have been writing about either the Finns or the Lapps when he described a primitive people he called the Fenni. Regardless, it is certain that by the first century A.D., the Finns were already in Finland and spreading. As they moved, they displaced or assimilated the Lapps who preceded them.

In about the ninth century, a Norwegian walrus hunter named Ohthera sailed to the White Sea, then up the Northern Dvina where he met the Beormas—a Finnish people who, he said, were smiths and spoke almost the same language as the Lapps. To the Scandinavians, English, and others who encountered them, these were strange, exotic people from the end of the world.

The Warrior Spirit of the Finns

As the Finns enter history, they are often seen as warriors. They served the Uppsala kings of ancient Sweden in Viking conquests south of the Baltic, and in the tenth century, Finnic Vikings known as the Ascomanni raided the Baltic and North Sea areas. Finns served the Byzantine emperors as bodyguards, palace police, and soldiers.

Much of this warring was forced upon them. After the Swedish King Eric the Good and the English-born Bishop Henry of Uppsala made Finland a province of Sweden, the Finnish homeland became known as the bloody shield of Sweden. The wars of the late Middle Ages were not gentleman's wars, but total, unrestrained fights for survival. Their fierce cavalry earned the nickname "Hakkapelis" from their battle cry—*hakkaa paalle*—which means "chop down the enemy."

This warrior spirit is not a thirst for blood, but rather a manifestation of indomitable will. There is a proverb among the Finns: strong will takes a person even through stone. The Finns call this will *sisu*, and more than anything else, it is this that characterizes the Finnish approach to life and magic. The word *sisu* is not translatable to other languages; it is uniquely Finnish perhaps because no other nation has felt such a great need for the quality. Sisu is not simply optimism or bravado, but rather a philosophy that what must be done will be done, regardless of the cost. This quality has preserved the Finns as a nation despite the fact that, for most of their recorded history, they had no government of their own. It has allowed them to survive forty-two wars with Russia—losing each one. It is a principle of integrity—the kind of integrity that compelled the Finns to pay their war debts even when wealthier countries chose not to. It is an indomitable will—this is the secret of their survival and also of their magic.

The Finnish warrior spirit is not one of belligerence or love of war. In fact, the Finnish national epic, the Kalevala, is the only national epic in which the central theme is not war. At the very end of the Kalevala, the great hero Väinämöinen sails away rather than engaging in conflict. The Finnish warrior avoids conflict, but when conflict is inevitable, the warrior enters into it with his or her whole being.

Wanderlust of the Finns

The ancient Finns were a nomadic or semi-nomadic society. Even when settled, Finns were fond of long voyages. This wanderlust led the Finns far from their Karelian homeland. This sense of wanderlust is present even in the Kalevala, which tells of Finns sailing to faraway places. Finnish Vikings traveled the inland waterways of Europe all the way to Black and Caspian seas, and some served critical roles in the founding of Russia. Evidence of their travel includes the discovery of early Arabic, English, and German coins found in Finland by archaeologists.

There were Finns who traveled with eleventh-century Viking Leif Erickson on his voyage to North America—including Thorfinn, the father of the first child of European parents in America. There were a significant number of Finns with the Russians at Sitka, Alaska, and Fort Ross in California. The seventeenth-century Swedish colony in the Delaware Valley known as New Sweden was peopled mostly by the Finns. There—in what is now New Jersey, Pennsylvania, and Delaware—the Finns transplanted their culture in America and brought with them the survival skills of the Savo-Karelian forest culture. In fact, much of what later became identified with the American frontier began in the forests of Finland.

Finns in America

Of the known settlers in New Sweden, the overwhelming majority were Finns. In the seventeenth century, there were ill feelings between the Swedes and the Finns, and Finns were often encouraged to leave. At the same time, Finns were also sought for the colony due to their reputation as woodsmen and outdoorsmen. When they arrived in America, the Finns found a very congenial climate and heavily forested fertile land. They also discovered that they shared much in common culturally with the Native Americans. The Swedes, on the other

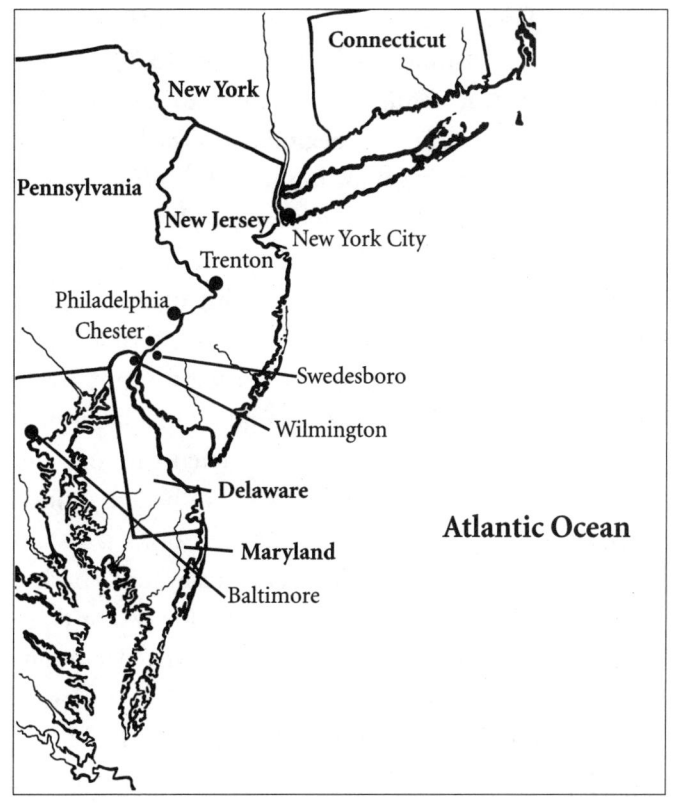

Map of the Delaware Valley

hand, found the area less to their liking and many of them returned to Sweden when given the chance. By 1664, the majority of the Delaware Valley population was Finnish. Few of the Finns returned to their homeland in northern Europe.

To a great extent, the settlement of the Delaware Valley was the transplanting of the Savo-Karelian culture. The Savo-Karelian Finns had, by this time, populated the interior of Finland. They had begun to settle the coniferous forests in central Sweden by about 1570, and the years of greatest Finnish movement to the Swedish forests were the thirty years beginning in 1600. The Savo-Karelians built one room log houses called *pirti*.

Their economy was based on agriculture, hunting, gathering, and fishing. They practiced *huuhta*, which involved the girdling, firing, and felling of trees to prepare a clearing for planting. The process took three years, which meant that the first harvest was not possible until the fourth year. They would plant a high-yield rye called *juurigen* that rapidly depleted the soil, and because of this, the land would have to be abandoned after the first crop. They also practiced *kaski*, a system of shifting cultivation when rye (juurigen), barley, turnips, oats, and flax would be grown for two or three years in clearings in the second-growth deciduous forests of alder and birch that grew after forty or fifty years of growth in old huuhta fields. The kaski and huuhta openings would be grazed and used to produce hay after they were no longer used for other crops. The practices of huuhta and kaski—in addition to hunting, fishing, and gathering—required a large territory and contributed to the continual movement of the Finns. The Finns would stay fifteen to twenty years at a farmstead before moving. It was a forest economy that required no draft animals or plows and was ideal for a pioneering people in a forested frontier.

The Finns and Swedes were the first to build log cabins in America—the English, Dutch, and Spanish had never built any such structures. C. A. Weslager writes that:

> *The facts are that no log cabins were built in Virginia until more than a century after the founding of Jamestown! And the log cabins in Georgia and the Carolinas came even later!*[1]

In fact, two trademarks of the Finns—the axe and the log cabin—became symbols of the American frontier. The Dutch and the English marveled at the ability of the Finns and Swedes to use the axe—one early English settler in the Delaware River Valley asserted that a Finn could cut down and prepare a log for a cabin in less time than any two Englishmen could accomplish the same task with a saw. In the Delaware Valley, the Finns again built pirti—cabins of logs with corner fireplaces—just as they had done for generations in Finland. In fact, the oldest log cabin still standing in North America can be seen today about five miles north of Swedesboro, New Jersey. It is known as the Nothnagle Cabin, so named for a subsequent owner, and is a registered national historic site. The Nothnagle Cabin is built of logs that are fully dovetailed with flush corners. There is a corner chimney and a fireplace made of bricks. It is now a wing of a frame house that was built sometime in the eighteenth century. Essentially, however, Nothnagle Cabin is a pirti.

I have heard the current owner of Nothnagle Cabin tell tour groups that the cabin was built by a Finn known as Antti Niilonpoika. I have been able to find only one source that questions Antii Niilonpoika's role as cabin builder; The Federal Writer's Project, Olin's *Finlandia*, and Esther Chilstrom Meixner's *Swedish Landmarks in the Delaware Valley* all attribute the cabin to Antii, who is often known by his anglicized name of Anthony Nelson. In a letter to Elmer Van Name, Mrs. Meixner wrote: "In Swedesboro, too, Anton Neilson, was the name given by those familiar with the house and its history."[2]

Connected with Anthony Nelson, the cabin takes on different importance—it is not simply the house of an early pioneer. Nelson was a constable, commissioner of lands, and colonial legislator. It is the workmanship of one of those who first built log cabins on this continent and in so doing, influenced the entire American frontier. It is a visible symbol of the birthplace of an American family: one of Anthony's sons built one of the most colorful of the early Jersey taverns, the Seven Star Tavern; other Nelson descendants fought in the Revolution, escorted Lincoln's body, and moved west as the nation expanded—and the family's story is not over yet. But perhaps most important for this story is the family's cabin as a symbol of magic and witchcraft.

In and around that cabin, Anthony and his family undoubtedly practiced other Finnish traditions—the sauna, playing the kantele, making clothes and shoes from birch bark. The songs and healing ways of the shaman would have been sung there by his mother,

Margaret Matson, who had been condemned by the English as a witch. We will hear more of Margaret's story later.

Across the Delaware River in Chester, Pennsylvania, in what was once known as Finlandia, is the restored cabin of Martti Martinen (Morton Mortonson). His grandson, John Morton, cast the deciding vote on the Declaration of Independence—merely voting to continue the independence the Finns had long felt. A few years later, John Hanson, another third generation American Finn, served as the first president of the United States under the Articles of Confederation. No wonder Franklin D. Roosevelt said:

> *From the beginning of our history onward, men and women of Finnish blood have played important roles in the development of our country. Their industry, stability, and resourcefulness have made them an important element in the American nationality.*[3]

Today, those of Finnish descent can be found throughout North America. Those earliest settlers have long since amalgamated with mainstream America—always doing what must be done to survive. Many intermarried with the Delawares, the Lenni Lenape. Finnish influence is seen by some in such Indian words as *Tamany* and *moccasin* (like the Finnish *muoksin*, a low leather-topped shoe).

Others left their name on the landscape, such as the Molucca River and Molucca Hill. Later, Finns immigrated to the Midwest and the northwest, and today the traditions of the old Finns continue in both the United States and Finland; the magical charms of old can be heard in the Midwest, and cabins built by Finns can be seen from Delaware to Oregon.

A memorial to the Finnish pioneers stands in a small park in Chester, Pennsylvania. Inscribed on one end of the memorial is a quote from the Kalevala that elegantly summarizes the Finnish pioneer experience:

> *Sons of Kalevala*
> *Far Sailing*
> *Passed an ocean's*
> *western reaches*
> *To this soil their*
> *strength applying*
> *On this shore*
> *A home established*
> *Toiled their crops*
> *To sow and garner*
> *Hewed their dwellings*
> *From the forest.*

Finnish Magic

The magic of the Finns was commonly believed by neighboring nations in former times. It was considered bad luck among sailors to kill a Finn. In the Middle Ages, Norwegian kings forbade their people to travel to Finnmark in order to consult magicians and during the sixteenth and seventeenth centuries,

Swedish authorities searched for and confiscated the *guodbas,* the magic drums of the Laplanders.

Scandinavians of the Viking Age considered the Finns and Lapps to be experts at magic—especially wind magic. The Norwegian Viking, Ingimud the Old, sent two Lapp shamans on a magic journey to find a silver image of Frey that he had lost. They described the location of the image in Iceland exactly where Ingimud was later to find it.

Richard Henry Dana recorded several conversations with sailors concerning the wizardry of Finns in the early nineteenth century. One sailor told of a Finn who kept a bottle "which was always just half full of rum, though he got drunk upon it nearly every day." The same reporter told of Finnish wizards controlling the wind:

> *He had heard of ships, too, beating up the gulf of Finland against a head wind and having a ship heave in sight astern, overhaul and pass them, with as fair wind as could blow, and all studding-sails out, and find she was free of Finland.*[4]

Many others have reported the Finnish wizards' ability to control the wind. Sir James George Frazer told of reports of Finnish ships making their way directly into a head wind. According to Frazer and other sources, the Finnish wizards would sell the wind enclosed in three knots. If the stranded sailors undid the first knot, they would receive a moderate wind. If they untied the second, they would get a gale. The third, when undone, would unleash a hurricane. The Estonians, whose country lies just south across the sea from the Finns, even in modern times have spoken of the magical powers of their neighbors. The Estonians typically attribute the bitter north winds to Finnish wizards and witches.

The Estonian belief in Finnish magic was preserved in a popular song:

> *Wind of the Cross! rushing and mighty!*
> *Heavy the blows of thy wings sweeping past!*
> *Wild wailing wind of misfortune and sorrow,*
> *Wizards of Finland ride by on the blast.*[5]

The Estonians, themselves, were believed to be magicians by non-Finnic people. One particular northern Estonian province was known as the land of wizards. People from other countries, especially Spain and Greece, were said to travel to ask questions of Estonian magicians.

Magic among the ancient Finns was pervasive. In fact, a person's status in society depended to a great extent on her or his magical power. It is no accident that the main characters of their national epic are all magi.

Finnish magic is firmly grounded in shamanism—the practice of using altered states of consciousness to influence the world and to acquire power. For the shaman, there are spirits in all things, and through these things they influence these spirits. The shamanism of the Finns is similar to that of other northern people including the Yakut, Chukchee, Samoyed, and other Siberian people. It is, of course, very similar to that of the Lapps, and even to that of the Eskimo.

Central to the practice of the Finnish shaman was the use of songs and chants. Great value was placed on knowing the right words and the stories of the origins of things. The mage sought knowledge from nature and the spirits that are found everywhere in nature. This knowledge could be passed down by others or gained through observation and experience—but the best source of knowledge was the shamanistic trance. The emphasis on magical knowledge can be seen in some of the terminology used—"wise woman" *(lointija)* and "knower of secret lore" *(tietäjä)*. These are similar to the meaning of the word *shaman,* which derives from the Tungus *saman,* which in turn is related to the verb *sa,* meaning "to know." In the Kalevala, magi are called "word-masters" and "wonder workers."

However, it is not the words alone that bring power. The mage applies that knowledge through an act of will. This involves the disciplined development of the mage through focus, practice, purification, and trance work. This self-development is clearly expressed in a passage from the Kalevala where Väinämöinen "made himself a maker, took the shape of a shaper."

The shamanistic trance involves the use of drums and songs and is similar to the shamanistic trances practiced by other people throughout the world. The trance is often preceded by the sauna, and at times the sauna itself is used as the instrument of trance. When seeking a trance or a shamanistic journey, the Finnish mages seek a sacred place such as the grave of a shaman when possible. This trance work, called God's hour, is best done in groups, but it can be done alone. Similarly, although chants are usually sung loudly and energetically, they can also be sung under the breath with great effectiveness.

Finnish magic is closely linked to daily life and practical activities. Väinämöinen, the central figure of the Kalevala, is not only a great magus, but also a proficient sailor and knowledgeable man who uses his magic for very practical purposes, such as transportation and agriculture. Ilmarinen is not only a magus but an expert smith who combines his magic and skill to create magical technology such as the Sampo. On one occasion, Ilmarinen created a woman out of gold in an episode reminiscent of the legends of Albertus Magnus' talking head and Kabbalistic legends of the golem. The Finns also used magic for divination and healing, and on at least one occasion, even used magic to stop an army with a song.

In the final analysis, the focus of Finnish magic is spiritual. The magus seeks to develop an awareness of the spiritual and of the spirits. Nature is full of spirits—not only animals and living things, but even inanimate objects are inhabited by spirits. Most of these have no name of their own and are named after the thing they inhabit. Others have proper names such as Tapio, Lord of the Forest and Tuoni, Lord of the Dead. These spirits are neither good nor evil, but they can, at times be helpful or mischievous. The attitude of the magus should be one of reverence toward all spirits and indeed all creation. At times this might appear as worship to the outsider, but is actually more a matter of courtesy and respect. For example, since Tapio is the Lord of the Forest, the animals were regarded as his herds. It was customary to ask for his permission before hunting and even promise offerings in return for a plentiful hunt. This is similar to what one would do if requesting the use of another mortal's property.

The focus of a sacred grove was a central sacred tree. In old Finland, one could find sacred groves, enclosed in fences, in which no wood could be hewn nor branches broken. Certain locations were felt to be particularly sacred because of the spirits who lived in or near them.

The spirits of the dead, especially one's own ancestors, were treated with reverence. The dead could not only influence the lives of mortals, but were sources of knowledge. For this reason, the graves of shamans were often chosen as sites for trance work. At these chosen sites, the shaman or *haltijat* would communicate with the dead. By dance and rhythmic chanting, the shaman's soul was able to cross the Otherworld River and enter the land of the dead—Tuonela. In the Kalevala, it tells how Väinämöinen went to the grave of Antero Vipunen, the ancient shaman, to seek magical knowledge. It is interesting to note that some identify Vipunen with Kaleva, the first ancestor of the Finns.

Above and beyond this multitude of spirits stands Jumala. Jumala is the greatest of all, the Creator, the Lord of Creation. He was the ancient Finnish thunder-god and the god of all the elements. Known at times as Ukko or the Old Man, Jumala is also called "god on high" and "Thunderer." Jumala is the name adopted by the

Christians in Finland for God. He is the chief and most frequently evoked deity in the Kalevala.

Although reverent of all creation—both material and spiritual—Finnish magic is no sour-faced pietism. It relishes life, love, and laughter. Self-effacing humor gives the mage the flexibility to survive in a world that is at times harsh and antagonistic.

The Finns were among the last Europeans to become Christian. As has often been the case, that process involved coercion as well as conversion—it should come as little surprise that the first Finn whose name we read in history is Lalli, who killed Bishop Henry of Uppsala in the twelfth century. The Finnish pagans were subject to persecution by the imperialistic policies of Medieval Christianity, and they responded in self-defense. Other Finnic peoples also resisted with violence. On St. George's Night in 1343, Estonian pagans attacked Christian churches and manors, killing priests and lay brothers. The Rebellion was suppressed by the Teutonic Knights, who in turn slaughtered thousands of rebels in revenge. The Mari and Udmurt, Finnic people in Russia, resisted conversion both to Islam and Christianity. As late as the 1870s in Russia, the Kugu Sorta—or Great Candle movement of the Mari—successfully resisted conversion to Christianity.

Resistance was not always violent, however. The Lapps, for instance, when forced to accept baptism, would wash the baptism away with chewed alder bark, sacred to the reindeer-god, Leib-Olmai. And in the *Saga of Olaf Tryggvason,* it is told how the Finnish sorcerer

Raud stopped the Christian King Olaf from entering a fjord by causing a storm to rise.

The persecution of the pagans continued in Sweden as it did in other countries, with the church's hostility toward magic and suppression of folk practices. This continued even across the ocean in New Sweden. Very early in the colony's existence we read of Karin, the witch. Karin was condemned for witchcraft and jailed, but managed to escape through magic. She was captured and jailed again to serve out her sentence. Centuries of violent oppression eventually resulted in dual faith practices and in the sublimation of traditional beliefs.

There is clear evidence that the traditional beliefs and practices continued with the Finns in the Delaware Valley colony. Among the early Finns in America was the family of Nils and Margaret Matson. Like many of the Finns, they had originally settled in central Sweden, where they were recruited to take part in the new colony. They traveled to New Sweden aboard the ship the Orn; the record of their voyage is a great adventure story. They were beset with storms and forced ashore in England and Calais. Later, they were stricken with disease that caused many to die. Many passengers became feverish and had to be restrained from leaping overboard to swim to the siren song of mermaids. So many were sick or dead that, by the time they were threatened by Turkish pirates, the few who were well propped up the sick and placed weapons in their hands to give the appearance of a well-armed ship. Fortunately, the pirates chose not to come closer. Other colonists traveling to New Sweden were not so lucky—many found themselves sold as slaves in North Africa or the Caribbean.

After Margaret and Nils arrived at Fort Christina, the Matsons settled farther up river in the area known then as Finland (near present-day Philadelphia) because of the large number of Finns who had settled there. When the Dutch attacked this Swedish colony, Nils and other Finns fought. Nils was taken to New Amsterdam as a prisoner of war and was later given a special citation by the colonial governor. The Matsons stayed after the Swedes abandoned the colony and together with the other Finns and Swedes who remained, they prospered with little interference from the Dutch. They were among the older settlers when William Penn arrived to take over his colony in the late 1600s.

Margaret Matson was known as a healer in the colony of New Sweden. Rumors of her being a witch had been spread since the days of Swedish rule. When the English took over, she found herself accused of witchcraft by her English neighbors. She had been accused of bewitching cattle—an offense that had led to the burning of witches in Sweden and England.

William Penn sat as the chief judge at her trial and, at one point in the trial, asked her if she had ever ridden a broom. To this she nodded yes. Penn, more enlightened than his fellow countrymen and contemporaries to the north in New England, said that he knew of no law against riding a broom in Pennsylvania. This was laughed at by some, and some considered Margaret mad. Others have implied an error in translation, since Margaret spoke Finnish and Penn spoke English. But in the Kalevala, Väinämöinen made a horse of straw and used magic to make it a means of transportation to a distant land. Similar practices can be found among the Siberian shamans in conducting shamanistic journeys. Perhaps that explains Margaret's response—perhaps she was affirming actual or astral travel through the use of magic.

Certainly, one who reads the complete transcript of Margaret's trial could not seriously consider her mad. Her self-defense was cogent and relevant. She challenged her accusers for offering hearsay evidence and presented herself as a rational and insightful woman. Penn found her guilty of having the "common fame of a witch," a reputation she'd had for many years, but she was not found guilty of the specific charges of bewitching cattle. She was put on probation for six months, and her husband and son were compelled to pay fifty pounds each to guarantee her good behavior.

Shortly after Margaret's trial, the family moved across the river to New Jersey, probably to avoid further persecution. It was there that her son, Anthony Nelson, built the cabin known today as Nothnagle Cabin, thus making the cabin a memorial to Finnish magic as well as to the contributions of the Finnish pioneers.

At the end of the Kalevala, Väinämöinen sails away leaving the land to the new king of Karelia, the newborn son of the virgin Marjatta. As he left he said:

> *May the time pass quickly o'er us,*
> *Let one day pass, let come another,*
> *And again shall I be needed.*
> *Men will look for me, and miss me,*
> *To construct another Sampo,*
> *And another harp to make me,*
> *Make another moon for gleaming,*
> *And another sun for shining.*
> *When the sun and moon are absent*
> *In the air no joy remaineth.*
>
> —Kalevala[6]

But the entry of Christianity did not mean the end of the old ways or the end of magic. As Väinämöinen sailed away, he:

> *Went upon his journey singing,*
> *Sailing in his boat of copper,*
> *In his vessel made of copper,*
> *Sailed away to loftier regions,*
> *To the sky beneath the heavens.*
> *There he rested with his vessel,*
> *Rested weary, with his vessel,*
> *But his kantele he left us,*
> *Left his charming harp in Suomi,*
> *For his people's lasting pleasure,*
> *Mighty songs for Finnish children.*
>
> —Kalevala[7]

Perhaps the most valuable legacy of Finnish magic is the appearance each Christmas of Santa Claus. Although his origins are in the story of Saint Nicholas, for some reason we have depicted Santa as a Finnish magus. He dresses in the fur-trimmed clothes and floppy pointed hat of the Finns and Lapps and drives a sleigh pulled by reindeer, as did Väinämöinen. He lives in the far north where, like Ilmarinen, he has a magical workshop. Santa Claus and Väinämöinen share a lust for life, a hearty laugh, and a great white beard.

And, like Väinämöinen, Santa is a traveler, the eternally ancient man, and a wonder-worker. Santa flies through the air by using magical reindeer, while shamans among all the northern Eurasian peoples were noted for the power of flight—sometimes flying astrally or through shape-shifting, but quite often they would fly through the use of magical horses or reindeer. The belief in flying reindeer is so ancient that it is even found in neolithic carvings.

Interestingly, the northern shamans achieved flight and the altered states of consciousness so central to their magic through the use of the *Amanita muscaria* or Fly Agaric mushroom. The Fly Agaric is notable for its bright red color and white spots. Could it be more than coincidence that these very colors are the colors of Santa Claus?

As the Finns live, so does Finnish magic. The songs of the shamans are still sung. The sauna is hot and alive. And they still apply their craft for the joy of the world. As it is said in the Kalevala:

> *If thy spells thou dost not teach me,*
> *All thy magic spells shalt teach me,*
> *Till no spells are hidden from me,*
> *Nor the spells of magic hidden,*
> *That in earth their power is lost not,*
> *Even though the wizards perish.*
> —Kalevala[8]

Endnotes

1. C. A. Weslager. *The Log Cabin in America: From Pioneer Day to the Present.* (New Brunswick, NJ: Rutgers University Press, 1969) 10.
2. Elmer G. Van Name. *Anthony Nelson Seventeenth Century Pennsylvania and New Jersey and Some of his Descendants* (Haddonfield, NJ, 1962) 3.
3. Aini Rajanen. *Of Finnish Ways* (Minneapolis, MN: Dillon Press, 1981), 210.
4. Richard Henry Dana. *Two Years Before the Mast* (New York: Collier and Son, 1909) 43.
5. James George Frazer. *The Golden Bough* (New York: Collier, 1922) 94.
6. *Kalevala: The Land of the Heroes,* trans. W. F. Kirby (London and Dover, NH: The Athalone Press, 1985), 645.
7. Ibid, 645–646.
8. Ibid, 210.

The Kalevala: An Epic of Magic

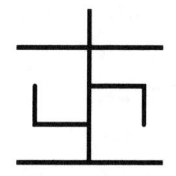

The Kalevala is the national epic of the Finns. Unlike the epics of other nations, the Kalevala is primarily a story of magic. While gods and wonders may play a role in other national epics, magic is central to the Kalevala, which contains a huge repertory of spells. The great quest of the heroes of the Kalevala is for magical power through the magical technology of the Sampo and by gaining power words from ancestral shamans or the underworld.

Without being preachy or authoritarian, the Kalevala teaches important values for the mage and for the children of Kaleva, the earliest ancestor of the Finns. The *-la* indicates possession, thus Kalevala means "of Kaleva," as in descendants or as in residents of the land of Kaleva. Among the values taught in the Kalevala are social responsibility and the futility of war. It also teaches a balance between environmental values and production. To anyone familiar with the Kalevala, it should not be surprising to find that these values are strongly held by the modern Finns and are even reflected in their national policies. The Kalevala also takes a stand against a materialistic lifestyle and speaks negatively of those who "scrape and fawn for silver." It is interesting to note that nineteenth and early twentieth century Finnish immigrants to America were often involved in the early labor movement and created communal societies inspired by the Kalevala.

The Kalevala reaches deep into the prehistory of the Finns. Its roots go back to the time of wandering before the Finns arrived in their northern home. It is a myth of creation and of the beginning of the world, time, and life. It is the saga of the Finnish forebears. It is a source of folk wisdom and culture. It is a collection of magic and shamanistic poems. Its vision is cosmic and epochal, but also particular and mundane.

The origins of the Kalevala are found in the oral traditions of the Finns. Its songs and stories were sung in isolated winter cabins in the sub-arctic forest. On those long nights, they would gather as families and friends and sing in the warmth and light. Those songs were their education. They were the means by which elders passed on the history and values of the ages or *muinaisuskoisia*, the word pertaining to ancient beliefs, usually translated as "mythical" in English. It was through those songs that they even passed on survival knowledge in woodlore, brewing, and agriculture.

Finnish Oral Tradition

The Finnish language was not written until the 1670s. The songs comprising the Kalevala are only a small portion of the Finnish songs that have been passed down orally, collected, and recorded. There are 22,795 lines in the Kalevala. Over 1,270,000 lines of stories and songs from the Finnish oral tradition have been published from the archives of the Finnish Literature Society, and many more remain unpublished. This wealth of poetry is a virtual treasure to those who want to understand the ancient ways.

Oral tradition depends on the memory of the storyteller or singer. Memory is aided by the poetry of the words and the rhythm of the songs. Memory is also aided by certain structural formulas, which also made composition of new verses easier. Such formulas are used in all folk traditions; two examples familiar to English-speaking readers are "once upon a time" and "they lived happily ever after." Such formulas are used most often to describe certain repetitive actions, including departures, grief, and magic. Because of their frequency and familiarity, they carry many emotional connotations and are especially useful in charms that rely upon mustering emotional energy.

The bards of old Finland, like those of other oral traditions, at times had memorized thousands of lines of poetry. One of the old bards sang continuously for two days and then told Elias Lönnrot, the compiler of the Kalevala, that as a child he would sometimes listen to his father and a friend sing all night for several nights in a row and never repeat a song. The old bard told Lönnrot that it would have taken many weeks to record all the songs that his father had known. He and other bards have indicated their belief that the oral tradition is dying out, and that in former days, the bards could remember much more than those of more recent times.

The oral tradition included presentation as well as form and content. In Karelia, the easternmost region of Finnish settlement bordering the White Sea, the usual manner of presentation consisted of two men sitting side by side with their right hands clasped. They would sway backward and forward in time with the rhythm. One of the men would act as the leader—main singer or *laulaja*—and the other as *säestäjä,* or supporting singer. Each in turn would sing the lines of the story. In Ingria, near present-day St. Petersburg, the songs were performed by groups of women who sang the songs as accompaniment for ring or long dances.

The word *laulaja* applies to either men or women. There were, of course, songs that in a sense were masculine and others that were feminine. But a male laulaja might sing feminine songs to create certain feelings, just as a female laulaja might sing masculine songs to sing of certain events.

These bards were also called *runo* or *runoi*, which meant singer of magic charms. The word came from an Old German word that meant a secret thing or magic charm, and came to indicate a character of the runic alphabet. Later, this word was used to indicate the major divisions of the Kalevala.

Contained within these runos are both greater and lesser traditions. The greater tradition, which formed the basis of the ritual life of the early Finns, involves the myths of creation and beginnings. It is sacred tradition containing profound wisdom and provides the basis for greater magical studies and spiritual growth. It is the central core of the epic.

The lesser tradition involves stories, folk wisdom, and charms. There is advice on daily living, including such things as housekeeping and beer making. There are sixty-five charms in the Kalevala, which include origin charms for various ailments and diseases, intimidation charms, fisherman charms, and conveyance charms. These charms, or *loitsurunot*, are representative of the day-to-day magic of the Finns.

In addition to the Kalevala, Lönnrot compiled the *Kanteletar*, a collection of lyric poems. The name can be translated as "Kantele-daughter" and is similar to the idea of muse in Greek mythology. The *Kanteletar* is more concerned with everyday life than is the Kalevala, providing the reader with great insights into Finnish culture. It also includes a considerable amount of ritual poetry.

The interesting thing is that the greater and lesser traditions are actually the same. As is true for many profound books, especially those that deal with the mystical and spiritual, the Kalevala can be read on many levels. It can be analyzed and philosophized, as is often the approach taken by scholars. It can be theologized, as is the tendency for some when approaching sacred texts. It can be approached with reverence and belief, as a metaphor with hidden meanings or read lightly and taken at face value. Each of these represents a valid approach, depending upon what we want to find.

Multiple interpretations are possible not only with texts, but also with experiences and people. The life of a great person from history, for example, can be taken as history, biography, or even as a metaphor or fable. Take the life of Abraham Lincoln. For some, he was one of many factors in a complex struggle. To others, he was larger than life—almost a saint. For still others, he is a lesson in tolerance, honesty, or persistence. This is the way with human experience, as well. Some of our own experiences can be dismissed as insignificant, while others become lessons for our children and their children.

The level of interpretation or approach to interpretation depends more upon our needs and approach than upon the nature of the text or experience. That which is most profound is often that which is most simple. The wise find wisdom everywhere.

The Father of the Kalevala

The chants and songs that comprise the Kalevala were collected by Elias Lönnrot. Born in 1805, Lönnrot became a physician. While still in college, he began his studies as a folklorist. From 1828 to 1844, he traveled on foot and skis from Northern Finland to the Karelian region gathering everything he could find about Väinämöinen, Ilmarinen, and Lemminkäinen. He collected variants from singers throughout Finland and compiled them into the epic poem. It is correct to call him the compiler, but not the author. He added nothing from his own head but used only the traditional songs he had collected.

In collecting and compiling the songs, Lönnrot was following the tradition of the old singers themselves, who would arrange the songs as they felt appropriate for a given performance and expand them with charms, lyrical materials, and proverbs as needed. The truly great contribution of Lönnrot is that he preserved this oral tradition for the first time in writing. Concerning his own role, Lönnrot said that, after realizing that his collection of songs far exceeded that of the most proficient singers, he decided that he had the same right as other singers to arrange the songs to tell a tale. Quoting the words of the songs themselves he said: "I began to practice magic, started to become a sorcerer." In other words he considered himself a singer of songs in the tradition of the bards and mages who created and passed on the tradition.

Despite great recognition for his contributions, Lönnrot preferred his peasant clothes and simple cabin. He sang the old songs, played the kantele, and enjoyed walking, swimming, and skiing until the very end of his life. He was noted for concentration, tolerance, humor, and unpretentiousness regardless of the situation. He was very much an example of the Finnish mage and a singer of great tales.

Overview of the Kalevala

The Kalevala is divided into fifty sections called *runos*. As previously mentioned, the word *runo* was formerly the name for a singer of magic songs and is directly related to an old Germanic word meaning a secret thing or a magic charm. In translation, the runos are sometimes called songs or cantos. Each runo can stand by itself, and they were traditionally sung individually or with other runos. The fifty runos can be divided into eight cycles. Each cycle focuses on a certain episode or character.

The dominant figure in the Kalevala is Väinämöinen. Väinämöinen is a mysterious and complex character who plays several roles in the epic. In the first cycle we read a story rich in symbolism, that tells of the birth of Väinämöinen from Ilmater, the Water-mother and creator of the world. Väinämöinen emerges as a water god and plays a role in the shaping of the world. In this same cycle, we read of Väinämöinen as Kaleva, the first man and a powerful shaman. To a certain extent, Väinämöinen is everyone. We read of his courtship and of his heartbreak. We read of his cleverness and humor, his pettiness and grief. We read of his success and his failure. His story is myth, and like all myths it brings the ritual participant into a sacred time to impart truth that transcends history.

Väinämöinen's primary role is that of shaman and mage. He is called *tietäjä iänikuinen,* or eternal sage. The Finnish word *tietäjä* indicates a knower of secret lore, hence a magician, wizard, or shaman. The word is used in the Finnish translation of the Bible for "wise man" or "magi." In the third runo, we find him in a magical battle with Joukahainen. The two mages meet and the young Joukahainen challenges Väinämöinen, "the oldest of magicians," to a duel, which consists of singing to demonstrate knowledge. Joukahainen sings, but makes little impression on the elder sage. After Joukahainen threatens to use physical force, Väinämöinen demonstrates his power and the superiority of magic over force. He sings, and his singing transforms Joukahainen's sledge and weapons into plants and stones. He sings Joukahainen into the earth until the younger magus relents and offers a bargain. This story strikes an interesting comparison with the Egyptian story of Setna. Setna wanted to steal a book of magic from the corpse of Nefer-ka-Ptah. Nefer-ka-Ptah awoke and asked if Setna would play a game for it. Nefer-ka-Ptah won the game and, through magic, caused Setna to sink into the earth.

In the Kalevala, we also read of Ilmarinen who, like Väinämöinen, plays several roles. Ilmarinen is, at times, seen as the sky-god, weather-god, and divine smith and at other times as a great shaman himself. He is referred to both as the brother of Väinämöinen and *takoja iänikuinen* or eternal smith. It was Ilmarinen who, as a god, forged heaven itself. He used magical tools made from his own clothes and used his knee as an anvil. Ilmarinen also makes the mysterious, magical tool called the Sampo. We read of his marriage to the Maid of the North and his grief following her death. We read of his prowess and skill when he creates a new wife from gold.

Lemminkäinen is the third major character of the Kalevala. He is an adventurer and is called *kaukomieli* or "man with a far-roving mind." But his mind is not just prone to travel and Viking raids. His appetites are for the softness and warmth of a woman's arms. His name probably derives from *lempi,* which is similar in meaning to the Greek Eros. He too is a mage, and we read of his singing enchanting the men of Pohjola.

Lemminkäinen enters into a number of tasks that include hunting the elk of Hiisi and bridling Hiisi's fire-breathing steed. Most notable of the stories of Lemminkäinen is one similar to the myth of the Egyptian Osiris. In this story, Lemminkäinen is ambushed and killed by an enemy from the north. His body is cut into pieces and thrown into the river of Tuonela. His mother uses a rake to recover the pieces, which she reassembles. She then restores him to life through magic.

The story of Kullervo begins with two brothers, Kalervo and Untamoinen, who from fabulous beginnings grow to head two great families. Kalervo settled in Karelia and Untamoinen in Suomi. They fought over fishing grounds. Then Kalervo planted oats before

Untamoinen's door, Untamoinen's sheep ate the oats, and Kalervo's dog ate the sheep. Enraged by this, Untamoinen swore to destroy his kindred. He mustered an army and waged war against his own brother. He massacred the clan, except for a lone pregnant maid. She was taken into Untamoinen's home where she gave birth to Kullervo, Kalervo's son.

From the cradle, Kullervo displayed remarkable strength. After three months, the child vowed vengeance for his father's death. Untamoinen feared him as the reincarnation of Kalervo and tried to kill him. Kullervo survived drowning and burning. Untamoinen had him hung from a tree. Kullervo not only survived, but carved the tree full of pictures of vengeance. At last, Untamoinen gave up his plans to kill the boy. Instead, he gave him a series of tasks. Kullervo purposefully failed by doing each task so excessively or brutally that he proved to be a useless slave and was finally sold by Untamoinen to Ilmarinen.

Ilmarinen's vicious wife mocked and mistreated Kullervo. She baked a stone in his bread. When he went to cut the bread he broke his knife, the only heirloom from his father, on the stone.

On the advice of a crow, he herded the wolves and bears from the forest and made them appear as cattle. When Ilmarinen's wife went out to milk the cows, she was attacked and killed by a wolf and a bear.

Subsequent to leaving Ilmarinen, Kullervo discovered that his father and mother had survived. He inadvertently commits incest with his sister. And, after some acts of devastating vengeance, he kills himself by falling on his own sword.

This rich, tragic tale calls to mind several parallels including the myths of Hercules. Most notably, Giorgio de Santillana and Hertha von Dechend have shown numerous parallels with the original legend of Hamlet, or Amlodhi. Both begin with the murder of the father by the brother, and Hamlet and Kullervo both vow vengeance and feign madness or incompetence as a means to their ultimate goal. Both stories involve raking embers and the motif of wolves changing to cows. Both involve the destruction of the Uncle's kinsmen and followers as well as incest. It is a story rich with deep insights and rooted in an ancient magical prehistory.

There is much more in the Kalevala, as well. There are voyages to Tuonela, the land of the dead; Viking voyages, romance and adventure; tragic beauty and comic joy. Whether read as literature, culture, myth, or magic, the Kalevala is a rich treasure.

The Sampo

The Sampo was a magical tool made by Ilmarinen at the urging of the northern witch Louhi. The esoteric nature of the Sampo is indicated by the materials from which it is made: a swan's quill tip, milk of a barren cow, a single grain of barley, and a single fleece of a ewe's wool. It is spoken of as a mill with a decorated lid that grinds out corn, salt, and money.

The Sampo is a rich symbol that can be interpreted on many levels. Culturally, it may represent the evolution from the Stone Age to Bronze and then Iron. In the process of making it, Ilmarinen makes first a crossbow, then a boat, a cow, then a plow. These represent the move through hunting, fishing, stock breeding, agriculture and then, at last, the Sampo. The link of technology and magic may seem strange to the modern mind, but it must be remembered that there was a time when these two approaches were one. As recently as the days of Queen Elizabeth I, we can see these two approaches combined in the person of the mage John Dee, and even later in the person of the physicist-alchemist Isaac Newton. As humanity moved from the Stone Age, they revered the newly discovered technology of metal as they revered the older technology of visions and spirits. In fact, they recognized the spirits of iron as they did the other spirits. It is not surprising, then, to find that many shamans used metal to decorate their magical robes. There are those who believe that the shamanism of smiths became the seed from which alchemy grew in later ages. Some have even proposed that the Sampo is actually a shaman's drum.

We read in the Kalevala that the Sampo was broken into pieces and lost. But even though broken, each piece was capable of marvelous power. Again, this can represent many things. The bards who sang these songs for Lönnrot said that these songs were part of a ritual for sowing grain. Within this story is the idea that nothing is ever lost. Our good deeds and our magical actions are like seeds that may lie dormant for a while, only to bring forth fruit at some later time.

The Sampo also has cosmological significance. It is the Cosmic Tree that holds up the heavens. According to Santanella, the Sampo represents Heaven itself. There seems to be some connection with the two constellations known as bears—Ursa Major and Ursa Minor. Altaic, a language family of Europe and Asia related to Finnish, has a similar word, *sumbar,* meaning "world mountain." Similarly, Sanskrit has *skambha,* which means pillar or pole. For the Finns and other ancients, the world was divided into three parts: the Upper World, the Middle World, and the Under World. The Cosmic Tree or World Pillar connected these worlds by holding up the sky and extending its roots into the Under World. It serves as a pathway between the worlds. In its branches can be found the spirits of those not yet born and in its roots, the world of the dead. Such a concept is found in the beliefs of most shamanic people.

For the Finns, this was both symbol and fact. In the sacred groves, one ancient tree was designated as the World Tree, representing the center of the universe and the path of the spirits. But this tree was more than a symbol. It was a place of power, and in a spiritual and psychological sense it was the center of the world. This was the tree that Väinämöinen left standing and where the eagle came to teach him. The eagle is often connected with ancient shamans and mages as a totem and as ancestor. A similar belief can be seen in the ancient Norse

Yggdrasill, and it is interesting to note that the ancient Norse shaman-god Odin was sometimes called Eagle.

The Sampo is the Holy Grail and Philosopher's Stone of the Finnish mages. It represents the ultimate happiness and prosperity of the people. It is the object of mystical search—the goal of wizards and alchemists. It is sought by warriors with sword and axe, but found only by mystics with magic and song.

Influence of the Kalevala

The Kalevala has been the single greatest influence on the formation and definition of modern Finland. This is not surprising when one realizes that it also represents the oldest and most unique traditions of the Finns. As the Finns emerged into history they soon became part of the kingdom of Sweden. Later, they were part of Russia. Although they retained their ethnic identity, they had no nation of their own. The publication of the Kalevala signaled the beginning of the Finnish nationalism movement that ultimately resulted in the formation of the modern country of Finland. Along with patriotism, many Finns also began to show greater interest in the old traditions. The traditions live on in hearts and lives, as well as on paper, largely because of the inspiration of the Kalevala.

Interest in the old traditions was more than superficial. Of course, there are probably a few who learned the old songs and how to play the kantele because it was fashionable. And there are some who probably grew full beards and built cabins in nostalgia for the old ways.

But there was also an awakening in many Finns of an awareness of important values. This led some to form cooperative farms—not just in Finland but even in America. And the impact on individual lives is perhaps a story that will never be sung.

The Kalevala has influenced great artists and musicians such as Akseli Gallen-Kallela and Jean Sibelius. It has been an influence on the written word as well.

Truth or Fiction?

Do the stories in the Kalevala have any basis in fact, or are they just fables made up to entertain and educate? The songs are true in the most important sense. They convey great truth. It is not necessary to believe that the world was created from a teal's eggs that fell from the lap of Ilmater to recognize the beauty and message of the runo of creation. The songs use poetic devices to illustrate points and create pictures. That does not make them less true.

The songs are true to their function. The singing of the songs brings us to a different time and place; a time when gods and men were closer, a sacred time. Entering that sacred time allows us to gain access to powers that are always there but remain unseen by those who have forgotten their past, their roots, and their connections.

The Kalevala is true in another sense, as well. It is the description of actual events, the history of actual people. The historical accuracy and incredible memories of the carriers of oral tradition are well documented. One of the more notable examples of both the antiquity and accuracy of oral tradition was noted by Gurdjieff in his autobiographical *Meetings with Remarkable Men*. In this source, Gurdjieff tells how he was raised hearing the oral traditions from his father, who was a bard. Later in life, he was surprised to read a magazine article that detailed the story of Gilgamesh, which had recently been discovered at Ninevah—his father had sung the very same story to him as a child. The story had been passed down, unchanged in oral tradition, through generations of bards for thousands of years.

The Kalevala is actually the story of Kaleva's children. Kaleva was the founder of the great family we know now as Finns. Little is known of him but his name; some have identified him with the ancient shaman, Antero Vipunen, whom Väinämöinen visited. He is remembered as a giant and a man of great power. The word *Kalevala* means Kaleva's district and refers to the land where Kaleva or his descendants settled.

The Kalevala is the story of the movement of Kaleva's children into their northern home. It tells of the disappearance of the sun and how the Dame of the North Farm took it from them—a description of the experience of the Finns as they moved far north and experienced the long absence of the sun during the northern winters. It tells of the interaction, hostility, and intermarriage of the Finns with the Lapps. It speaks of cultural change and of survival. The ancient Greek philosopher Euhemerus proposed that the gods were men whose stories had grown in the telling. In part, that is the truth of the Kalevala.

This is not to say that it is fiction or fable. Was there a magical duel between Joukahainen and Väinämöinen? I have no reason to doubt it. There had to be many duels between the shamans of the Lapps and the shamans of the Finns. Did old Väinämöinen visit the land of the dead? Certainly. That is a primary activity of shamans in every culture. These events occurred not once but many times. In the life of every person there is laughter, love, heartache, tragedy, triumph, and unexpected coincidence. The more individual the experience of truth is, the more universal it is. That is the truth of the epic of Kaleva's children. That is the truth of the magic of the Finns.

The World of Spirits

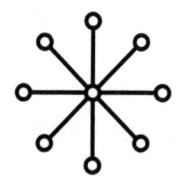

Basic to Finnish magic is the understanding that the world is composed of spirits. Every object, plant and creature has a spirit, which in Finnish is called *haltija* and means ruler. These spirits vary in intelligence, power, abilities, and motivations—just as do humans. But, though they may vary in many areas, each is an actual being who feels, thinks, perceives, and interacts with the surrounding world.

The haltija is not a spirit as is usually understood by western religion or philosophy. That is to say, it is not some immaterial "other." It is not a formless, shapeless force or immanence. It is actually part of the structure and being of anything and everything that exists. It does not exist apart from, but rather as part of each thing in the world.

A rock, for example, has an haltija. Depending on the rock it might be friendly or not so friendly. Some may have more power. Some have less. Certain rocks may be easily persuaded to assist the mage. Others may resist or impede the mage's efforts. So it is with everything.

This is not to say that rocks see or think as humans do, but it is not to say that rocks do not perceive or think either. Does your pet dog or cat think and feel? Only the most rigid Skinnerian behaviorist would say no. But does your pet think and feel as you do? For that matter, do you think and feel as any other being—human or non-human? To say that there are differences in quality or style in no way proves the absence of spiritual qualities.

Of course, to help us understand the haltija of other things we speak and think anthropomorphically. We refer to them as though they were human. We speak of them walking and speaking. We refer to their limbs and eyes. This is all metaphorical, but it is useful because it gives us a way of speaking. It should not be understood literally. We all speak of the sun rising and setting, even though we know that it is an illusion caused by the earth's rotation. Similarly, we can speak anthropomorphically of the haltija simply to facilitate speech and understanding.

That is not to say that some haltija are not in the form of humans, or at least may appear that way. There are some which choose to manifest themselves in human form from time to time. Others do not have that ability. Again, this shows how there are great differences among the spirits.

The haltija should not be understood dualistically, as in western philosophy. There is not a spiritual world and a material world. There is a world. The world and the things of the world are composed of many parts. The human body for example has bones, blood, nerves, skin, and a number of organs. None of the parts is a human, nor is a human complete without each part. Similarly, the haltija and the body are both essential to a complete being—whether human, rock, plant, or animal.

This does not mean that the haltija does not have an independent existence. Elements are elements. They exist whether combined into one form or another or when unorganized and awaiting development into something else. On the other hand, it would be incorrect to assume that the haltija alone is responsible for the character of any being or thing. The character of a thing is a synergistic reaction between the haltija and the body—just as water is the synergy of hydrogen and oxygen.

In general, the haltija is the source of intelligence and volition. In varying degrees, all things from the smallest subatomic particle to the greatest sun, from the smallest microbe to the greatest whale, have intelligence and volition.

To gain power the mage must learn the nature of things. The knowledge sought involves practical material things and the nature and origin of the haltija. This latter knowledge can be gained to a small degree from other mages, but is gained from the spirits themselves. This search for understanding is, in great part, the object of Finnish magic.

In addition to the haltija, animals and humans have a spirit or life force called *löyly.* This is derived from the word for breathing and is similar to the Hebrew *ruach* or the Greek *pneuma,* which both indicate spirit, wind, or breath. The connection of löyly and breath or wind is also seen in the old Finnish belief that the departure of the löyly at death can cause a storm or gust of wind. It is the löyly that the magus sends out in astral projection. This projective ability is not limited to the human soul. Everything has a löyly or soul that can be freed from the object itself. When it is sent out, it is sometimes called the shadow and is perceived by others as the form of the magus. Although it is most often a human form, it sometimes manifests in animal form such as a bat, mouse, or gray butterfly. It can also manifest as a beetle, bird, wolf, or caterpillar. The shadow can leave the body at sleep, and at death it may appear as a whirlwind or as a blue flame from the ground.

This shadow spirit can be so highly developed that it acts as a spirit guide to the mage. This tutelary spirit is known in Finnish as *varjohaltia* (shadow ruler) or *saataja* (guide). It can predict the future and warn the mage of danger. It can also precede the very powerful magus as a *haamu* or shadow-soul, similar in concept to the *doppelganger* in Germanic myth. Without löyly there is no life, but it is the haltija that controls both body and löyly.

All spirits should be recognized and treated with respect. This attitude of reverence is most often exhibited in acts of courtesy. For the Finnish mage, it is only proper to ask permission when intruding in the space of others or when using the resources of others.

An attitude of reverence obligates the mage to conserve and protect. No life should be taken needlessly, no resources should be squandered. The old Finnish tradition of pouring back two drops so that a well will not die reflects this reverence.

But all spirits—just as all people—are not friendly. There are those who are malicious or mischievous. Although courtesy and mutual respect are the preferred path, there are times when other strategies are the safer course. The mage might wisely choose to avoid an enemy. In other cases, caution might be exercised by forming alliances, taking protective measures, or even by conflict. An example of this principle is the tradition of protective charms, such as when a Finnish sailor would throw a coin into the water and say "May I be as light as a leaf and Nakki as heavy as iron." This was intended to provide protection from the malicious water spirit, Nakki.

Talismans are used to control haltija. Their effectiveness relies of course on the knowledge and power of the individual mage, but also upon the character of the specific spirit involved.

Chants are used to communicate with the haltija. This communication is similar in quality to any interpersonal communication. Chants relay information, make requests, and invoke feelings. Most often the mage chants in order to find out the origin of things.

The Gods

For the Finnish mages, spirits can be understood as powers of nature that are animate and capable of decisions. These spirits differ in their abilities, just as do mages. In general, they can be perceived as more or less on the same plane as humans. But there are greater spirits as well. They transcend the abilities of the "natural" plane. They do not differ in essence from other haltija, but through their age, effort, experience, or journeying they have gained greater knowledge and power. They are not one-dimensional, they are rather complex individuals with unique personalities. Many of the gods are literally our divine ancestors and so may be referred to as "old ones," "fathers," and "mothers," as well as gods.

The gods are representations of power. However, this does not mean that they are not real. It merely reminds us that the gods are not as we conceive of them, but rather as they are. We personify these powers in order to better understand them and relate to them. This was done by many ancient peoples through the use of totems. A totem—a bear, for instance—is not the bear itself, but instead the powers and traits that are represented by the bear. This does not detract from the reality of the gods; they are real and powerful. They also have personal traits, intelligence, and even personalities. When approached with the proper attitude, they can help the mage develop personally and gain access to needed resources and tools.

The gods of the ancient Finns fall into three principle categories. This is understood best by picturing the World Tree and its three parts: Underworld, Middle World, and Upper World. These are not to be understood in terms of the Christian hell, earth, and heaven, nor as an alternative to that belief. These worlds represent alternative states of consciousness or aspects of the human psyche as well as aspects of the world of nature.

Celestial Gods

The greatest deity in the Finnish pantheon is Jumala, the supreme god and creator. His sacred tree is the oak. For some he is perceived as the ultimate deity—a god-principle from which everyone and everything else derives life and being. Others perceive him as identical with Ukko, the sky or thunder-god. Both perceptions are true. Jumala is the transcendent power that allows gods to be gods. Jumala gives life and being to everything; he is the supreme creative principle. Jumala is pure, asexual, transcendent intelligence and energy.

But Jumala is also a being—infinitely advanced in knowledge, wisdom, and power—but a being nonetheless. Jumala is the most advanced example of the god-principle known to this world. Jumala has a body, feelings, sexuality, and personality.

Jumala was worshipped by all the Finno-Ugric people under various local names: Taevataat ("Sky Grandfather") in Estonian, Jumo in Mari, Inmar in Udmurt, and Ibmel in Lapp are a few examples.

In ancient times, the Finns worshipped Ukko Ylijumala by throwing löyly in the sauna. Ukko, together with his wife, Akka, created humanity. Ukko was responsible for the soul, the haltija. Akka was responsible for the body. She guarded the harvest and fertility. Akka is also known as Rauni from the mountain ash, which is her sacred tree. The holy wedding of Ukko and Rauni was celebrated in the spring with sacrificial festivals involving drinking and pouring drinks, as well as sexual activity.

Other celestial gods include Paiva, the sun; Kuu, the moon; Otava, the Great Bear; and Ilma, the divinity of the air. Thunder was worshipped as Isanen, "the little father," or as Ukko, and usually identified with the Norse god Thor. Ilma's daughter, Luonnotar, was Väinämöinen's mother. Also mentioned in the Kalevala are Kuutar, the daughter of the moon and Paivatar, the daughter of the sun. In Lapland, the sun, Pieve, was seen as feminine and was represented as a circle or lozenge with four rays. The moon, Mano or Aske, was seen as masculine and represented as a crescent.

Norse Gods

Several Norse gods were also known to the Finns, most notably perhaps were Odin and Thor. Odin, also known as All-Father, was the ancestor and leader of the Aesir.

He was also the national god of the Lapps or Saami, to whom he was known as Rota.

Odin was most likely an historic personage who led the Aesir from Asia Minor into Scandinavia. There he assumed the ritual name of Odin, which is related to the Old Norse "Od," meaning wind or spirit. He then founded a priesthood of twelve wise men. He was a tall, thin man with a long cloak and grey hair to his shoulders. He was a one-eyed shaman and a shapeshifter. His single blue eye was striking and his empty socket was hidden under a hood. He was sometimes known as Grim, from the Old English for hooded or masked. He carried a blackthorn staff and often wandered the earth accompanied by a raven and wolves. Among his more memorable feats was causing the decapitated head of Mimir to speak. His burial site is said to be near the site of his major shrine in Uppsala, Sweden.

Central to his story was his search for mystical knowledge. For nine days and nights he hung pierced by his own spear, Gungnir, on Yggdrasill, the World Tree, in order to win the secret of the runes. He paid his one eye in order to drink sacred mead from the cauldron of inspiration owned by the god Mimir. These myths undoubtedly refer to the practice of some shamans of using pain as a path to shamanic ecstasy, another familiar example of this is the Sun Dance of the Lakota Sioux, which also teaches the value of self-sacrifice in the pursuit of mystical knowledge and perfection.

The runes or mysteries became central to the rituals of the cult of Odin. They represent ecstasy, poetry, and magic. Rune masters considered themselves to be blood relatives to Odin. Runes are more fully discussed in the chapter "Symbols of Magic," beginning on page 139.

The Odinic Mysteries involved an initiation ceremony reminiscent of those of the Gnostics. In the Odinic Mysteries, Baldur was the central figure moving through a series of gates, learning certain signs and knowledge. A major focus of the Odinic rituals is self-sacrifice. The ritual took place in a series of nine caverns, which represented the nine worlds of the spirit and nature. The initiate took on the role of Baldur and moved from cave to cave in a dramatic ritual that involved oaths and the imparting of sacred knowledge. At the end of the journey, the initiate entered a sacred room with a roof that was lined with battle shields. He took an oath of secrecy and swore allegiance to Odin. There, he kissed the naked blade of a battle sword and drank mead from a cup that had been made from a human skull. He was given a silver ring carved with runic characters and told that he had passed through death and had been reborn as a perfect being.

The berserkers, Norse warriors and initiates of the Odinic cult, were often shapeshifters. Bothuar Bjarki, the champion of King Hrolf of Denmark, fought in the form of a bear and wore skins of animals. Connected to this is the bear cult, which was widespread throughout northern Eurasia and played a role in the cultures of all Finnic people.

Odin has been identified with Hermes or Thoth. Odin wore a slouched hat and Hermes too wore a hat. Both were known as mages and were linked to the invention of writing. Both were considered psychopomps, guides for the dead. Both were known to fly through the air. Both were founders of mystical traditions. The Hermetic tradition, like the Odinic mysteries, involved ritual ceremonies, initiations, and occult knowledge.

Odin, like the shamans of Siberia, used an eight-legged steed. Odin would ride his steed, Sleipner, through the air and into the world of spirits. He was also known to send forth his spirit as a bird, fish, beast, or dragon while his body would lay as if asleep or dead. He was the god of storms, and it was sometimes thought that his messages could be heard in the winds. Although a Norse god, his shamanic connections make him a natural ally to the Finnish deities.

The Norse god Thor can be found among all the western Finno-Ugric peoples including the Finns, Karelians, Estonians, and Lapps. The Lapps called him Horagalles or Old Man Thor. To the Estonians, he was Tooru or Taara, and Torym to the Ostyaks. It is also interesting also to note that Thursday, or Thor's day, was the holy day of the old Finnic pagans.

Thor was noted for his hammer, Mjollnir. Mjollnir was also called Killer of Giants and Smasher of Rocks. The hammer is so closely identified with Thor, that a hammer or two-headed ax is often used as his symbol. The hammer of Thor and pictures of Thor himself were frequent symbols on the drums of Finnish shamans. In addition to Mjollnir, Thor also wore a belt of power that doubled his strength, and iron gloves worn to grasp Mjollnir.

Frigg, also called Frigga, was the wife of Odin. She was the goddess of fertility and sexuality. Her symbol is the distaff, with which she weaves destinies.

Freya, the goddess of love, is often confused with Frigga, just as love is often confused with sex. Freya was a shaman noted for her psychic powers and shapeshifting. She was the patron of a female priesthood known as the *volvas*, who were renowned for their prophetic utterances. Volvas had familiars in the shape of cats—the totem of Freya. It was Freya who imparted the rune knowledge to Odin.

Frey is the god of fertility and the consort of Freya. They are also brother and sister. He is ruler of the elves, fairies, and goblins and presided over the celebration of the harvest.

Baldur, who was mentioned in conjunction with the Odinic mysteries, is the son of Odin and Frigg. Baldur inherited from them wisdom and a love of nature. He was the most beautiful of the gods, with long blonde hair and striking blue eyes. Odin engraved his tongue with speech runes, making him the most eloquent of the gods, as well. He was very popular and often acted as a peacemaker by resolving disputes among the gods.

Baldur's popularity and beauty caused him to be resented by Loki, the god of fire, divine trickster and brother of Hel, the Queen of the Dead. Loki plotted against Baldur, but Frigg heard of his plot and made all living things swear an oath that they would never harm Baldur. She overlooked mistletoe, however, and did not cause it to make the promise. Mistletoe had been ignored because it clung to the oak and had no power of its own. To prove Baldur's invulnerability, Frigg had the other gods throw spears at him and strike at him with their swords. Baldur was unharmed even when mighty Thor struck him with the great hammer, Mjollnir. But Loki tricked Frigg into telling him that the mistletoe had not taken the oath. Loki then took a sprig of mistletoe and, with the help of an elfin smith, fashioned it into an arrow. Loki took the arrow to the blind god Hothar and encouraged him to join in the fun and shoot an arrow at Baldur. The arrow went into Baldur's heart and he died. Loki confessed and was condemned to be chained to a rock for eternity while a snake spat venom in his face.

Divinities of Earth and Waters

The gods of nature are as numerous and varied as the displays of nature, herself. There is Pellervoinen, the protective god of fields and lord of trees and plants. The Mother of Metsola personifies the forest. Suonetar is the goddess of blood veins. Even the bee, Mehilainen, is respected as a messenger. Nature spirits are often thought of as having a mixed appearance. For example, a forest spirit might appear as a beautiful woman in front, but in the back appear as a tree trunk or an animal. Bronze amulets, which portrayed human figures with the head of moose, have been found from among the ancient Chud people. The Lapp god Radien Kiedde is portrayed as a man with antlers.

Frequently the gods are seen in family groups, particularly forest spirits. Tapio of the dark beard, the fir bonnet, and moss cloak, together with his wife Mielikki and their son Nyyrikki and daughter Tuulikki are deities of the woods. They are invoked to assure an abundance of game.

Ahto or Ahti is the chief water god. He, his wife Vellamo, and their daughters are surrounded by numerous spirits of the waters. Many of these lesser spirits are harmful, like Vetehinen and Tursas. The hero, Lemminkäinen, also bore the name Ahti and is probably the same as the water god.

The fish-god is usually represented as having a human head with long hair and the lower body of a fish. It is interesting to note that as late as the seventeenth century, belief in mermaids and mermen was common among Finns. During the voyage of the Orn to America in 1654, which carried Nils and Margaret Matson, many of the passengers stricken mad with fever leaped to their deaths in order to reach the long-haired mermaids with the beautiful voices.

Water spirits were often perceived as evil or destructive. Spirits of drowned people, if seen, were believed to be omens of misfortune. Some water spirits could bewitch humans with their singing. The spirit of the water itself, Veden Haltia, is believed to go bad if it leaves the water.

House spirits, on the other hand, are single, though in another sense they were members of the family. The house weasel was thought to bring luck to the household, and especially for horses. The cricket was thought to be the herald of the house spirit and house snakes would suck up the earth's wrath. House spirits in general increased happiness and were sometimes present as real pets. The house spirit can sometimes be heard as voices, sounds, or knocking.

The house father is seldom visible, but at times appears as a white haired or mousy gray haired bearded man. This particular spirit might also take a feminine form as house mother. In addition to the house spirits, there are also yard spirits, the fire mother, hearth mother, and sauna spirits. These spirits can be petitioned to help with wishes and prevent misfortune. Elementary magical means are often used with these domestic spirits. Such things as sayings, charms, and simple rituals can be used to incorporate the spirits into the daily routine of the household and ensure their good will.

Closely associated with the house spirits are the various earth spirits. The earth goddess is usually not given a definite form, but she is perceived as having human characteristics. Her worship involved the building of labyrinths, which symbolize the divine womb and the love and security of the goddess. The Kalevala mentions how Kullervo built such a labyrinth. There is also a wall painting of the goddess in the labyrinth in the church at Sibbo, Finland. Goddess worship was also involved with the ancient amber trade that connected the Baltic Finns with the Mediterranean Greeks.

There are also many evil spirits on the earth. They are mischievous at best, at worst malicious. The footsteps of forest devils will sometimes be heard even though they cannot be seen. Three such evil spirits—Lempo, Paha, and Hiisi—combined their powers together to injure Väinämöinen. While the mage wielded an axe, Hiisi made the handle shake when Lempo turned the blade toward Väinämöinen. Paha caused the blow to go amiss. Together they caused the axe to cut deeply into the mage's leg. Grain-maidens and the rye-wolf were said to damage crops and frightened people. Such evil and mischievous spirits were not worshipped, but could be rendered harmless through such magic as charms.

The Underworld

The land of Tuoni, Tuonela or Manala, is the land of the dead. But Tuonela is not a place of punishment, it is merely another plane of existence. It is darker there, but the sun shines and forests grow. It is a distant land—a long march one week through thickets, another week through woods, and a third week through deep forests. It is protected by a dark river. There is the isle of Manala, the land of the dead. It is said that many enter Tuonela, but few come out again.

Lemminkäinen went there to satisfy the sorceress Louhi. There, to fulfill his quest, he shot the swan of Tuonela. He was then slain on the banks of the dark river. His body was torn to pieces, but he was miraculously resurrected by his mother's magic.

In the Kalevala, only Väinämöinen returned from Tuonela unharmed. He journeyed there in search of magic words—the archetypal shaman's journey to the Under world—the shaman journeys to Tuonela in search of power and to learn from the spirits. It is the land of the dead, the land of dreams and the place where we find the collective unconscious mentioned by Carl Jung.

Tuoni is Lord of the Under world. Ruling with him is his wife Tuonetar. Their daughters are divinities of suffering. They are Kipu-Tytto, the goddess of illness and Loviatar, the source of all evil with her black and horrible face. Loviatar and her husband, the Wind, had nine monsters as children: Scabies, Ulcers, Phthisis, Gout, Colic, Pleurisy, Canker, Plague, and a fatal spirit that is eaten up with envy who has no name.

Death is personified by Kalma, who reigns over graves—the word *kalma* in Finnish means the odor of a corpse. On Kalma's threshold dwells the monster *surma*, the personification of fatal destiny or violent death. Associated with Kalma are the goddesses of pain and disease, including Kivutar and Vammatar.

There was also a belief in other subterranean spirits that are like the dwarves of other traditions. They were believed to be very small but possessed of great supernatural strength.

Ancestors

Of major importance to the Finnish mages are the haltija of ancestors. The living and dead members of a family have a reciprocal relationship. The living can gain wisdom and protection from the ancestral spirits, while the ancestral spirits gain substance and organization from the attention of the haltija of their embodied offspring.

Those who have gone before do not lose interest in the affairs of their loved ones, and in fact, extend their love over generations. Their protective intervention can provide comfort and guidance in times of emergencies. They are able to intercede with other haltija, and even gods, on behalf of their families. They can also appear in dreams and trances to instruct their descendants. These protective spirits are known in Finnish as *saataja* and are similar to the western Christian concept of guardian angels.

The ancestral spirits are able to remain in touch with this plane of existence, but over a period of time they become increasingly detached. They can lose all interest in the affairs of this world, even to the point of losing their identity. This detachment can be stopped or even reversed through the reverent attention of the living. For this reason, those ancient ones who headed large clans often remain as powerful spirits or even gods. These ancient ones include Odin and Väinämöinen.

The ancestors are honored in three ways. First, to honor them we must know them. It is not enough, however, to simply find out their names, birthdates, and other basic genealogical data. We must learn as much about them as possible. We must learn the stories from their lives. Second, we must tell their stories. In this day and age, those stories should be written and shared among the living family, they should be told at gatherings. Third, the ancestors should be honored and remembered through ancestral rituals, which will be discussed more fully in a later chapter.

Respecting the Gods

The gods, and all haltija for that matter, deserve our reverence. With the exception of Ukko Ylijumala, they are not worshipped in the way westerners usually think of worship. They are honored and respected as beings of great power and knowledge.

To respect the gods we must have awareness of the sacred in all things, and we must show respect. This is most often done by addressing the divine in the things we use and in the places we go. The ancient Finns would address the gods of the forests and rivers. The modern sage might address the gods of machines or tools. Finnish hunters would not kill without reason and would not leave wounded animals. These simple ceremonies of permission and thanks are the essence of respect.

There are also occasions for more elaborate shows of respect. There are special days and can be honored with feasts and festivals.

There are special places—sacred places—recognizable to the aware by the almost tangible feelings of sacredness they emit. Care should be taken to avoid these places except to perform sacred activities. Under no circumstances should they be desecrated by acts of violence, destruction, or uncleanness. Whenever possible they should be clearly marked with a fence or other barrier.

Altars and icons are also used to designate sacred places and to show respect. Altars can be places of sacrifice and forums for communication. These are more fully described in the chapter "The Magic of Nature."

To respect the gods is to communicate with the gods. Acknowledge them openly, just as you would recognize a friend on the street. Give them respect. Ask their permission if it is needed. Give them thanks when it is due. Gifts help to build the relationship and firm the bond.

Trance Work
and Ritual

Finnish magic is, above all else, pragmatic. Do what works. The mage is not bound by traditional or established ritual. The most powerful magic is a result of spontaneity and creativity rather than of strict adherence to a set pattern.

Ritual magic usually begins with music. This could be song, chanting, or instrumental music. Ritual will also frequently involve some action—gestures or dancing. It always involves the attention and imagination or the mage.

One of the important functions of ritual is to induce altered states of consciousness through trance. Ritual both induces changes in consciousness and marks these changes. It is during such trance states that the mage gains access to other levels of reality to learn secrets of magical power and to effect changes in the world.

Trance can be used at any time. It is certainly appropriate for marking important times such as equinoxes, solstices, new moons, full moons, midsummer, and ancestral dates. It can be entered spontaneously as the need is felt and can also be performed at regularly scheduled times. To maximize the effects of trance, it should be used frequently.

Frequent use of magical rituals increases the mage's ability to move rapidly between states of consciousness. Practice also increases the mage's understanding and abilities. It is through experience with trance that the mage is able to perform rituals powerful enough to cause changes in the world. Trance work and rituals come to work together.

Preparation

Life is the preparation for ritual. Ritual is merely the focusing of the mage's personality so as to effect change. Thus, the mage should live a magical life, which would include a number of characteristics: courage, attention, compassion, spontaneity, intuition, imagination, playfulness, and of course, sisu.

The key to the development of these and other qualities is awareness. Simply consciously choosing to think about certain qualities increases their strength. A very simple and useful exercise is to begin each day by focusing briefly on a certain quality that you wish to strengthen. Visualize exactly how you expect this quality to be manifest. Effort should then be made during the day to notice evidence of that quality and to practice.

Certain qualities can be increased through purposeful exercise. Here are two exercises that are particularly useful when preparing for magical rituals.

Exercise One
Simply notice your sensory experience. Notice the feelings of texture and pressure against your skin. Notice how things look—color, shape, shading, size, depth. Notice sounds and the absence of sounds. Be aware of smells and tastes. Really notice them. Be aware of feelings inside your body as well as outside your body. Notice how your breath feels as you inhale and exhale.

Exercise Two
The second exercise follows from the first. Sit quietly and mentally recreate the sensory experiences of the earlier exercises. Mentally experience the feelings, sights, smells, and other sensations in every detail and aspect that you experienced earlier.

Rituals

To be most effective, rituals should involve several qualities. First, they must involve the complete mental attention and emotional focus of the mage. The mage must prepare and hone that focus through meditation and other exercises. The material elements of the ritual should be chosen carefully so that they will help rather than hinder focus. The setting and timing also become a very important element to consider. The ritual should incorporate multiple symbols that draw in the mage's understanding at different levels. The symbolism should also appeal to as many sensory modes as possible.

Rituals should be both spontaneous and well planned. Planning will help the mage to invest the symbolism with emotion and will increase understanding of the meaning of the ritual. However, no ritual should be so rigidly performed that it excludes immediate inspiration. Rituals, after all, are a method for entering trance and communicating with the spirits. It would be disrespectful to ignore their input.

The basic ritual begins with an invocation, which can be either spoken or sung. All gods and spirits that might have an interest in the outcome of the ritual should be called upon. Respect can be shown with proper titles and through the recitation of significant qualities. This should be followed by a period of quiet. The next phase should be a period of recital or reading—material can include appropriate passages of the Kalevala, Nordic sagas, or poetry.

The main body of the ritual then follows. This will vary according to the type and purpose of the ritual. A hunting ritual, for example, often involved the ritual acting out of a successful hunt. Other rituals include the sauna, sacrifices, making runes, creating magical tools, dancing, and singing. A ritual might consist of making a picture that embodies some material or spiritual objective. It also involves making a fire or lighting a candle, followed by burning petitions to the gods. Another common ritual would be sharing a meal. The action can be done in silence or accompanied by words or song. Regardless of the exact nature of the ritual, it should involve and facilitate trance through the focusing of the mage's attention and emotions. The ritual proper is then often followed by further recitation or reading. Finally, thanks are given to the spirits and gods.

Summary of the Basic Ritual
1. Invocation. Call upon all the spirits and gods who might need to be interested in the outcome of the ritual.
2. A period of quiet meditation.
3. Recite or read appropriate sacred words from the Kalevala, Nordic sagas, or poetry.
4. Conduct the main portion of the ritual.
5. Recite or read.
6. Give thanks to the spirits and gods.

Focusing

Trance begins with focus. Choose a quiet place with dim lighting to minimize distractions. You may find that music—particularly drumming or chanting—will help you focus, but it is not absolutely necessary. Even if music or dance are used, the same fundamental principles apply.

Practice focusing on externals. Appropriate objects of focus include sounds such as drums and sights such as natural scenes and magical symbols. Also practice focusing on internals. Particularly useful internal objects of focus include one's own breathing, pleasant images and physical sensations.

Basic Trance

Lie down on your back or your right side. Close your eyes. Notice where you feel warmth and relaxation. Wonder where that relaxation and warmth will be felt next. Now focus on your breathing. Notice that the more deeply you breathe, the more relaxed you become.

If you prefer, you can sit or kneel instead of lying down. Focus on an external object such as a tree, an interesting piece of wood, or a sacred stone. Notice the sensations in your legs and shoulders. Notice where there is warmth and relaxation. Wonder where that relaxation and warmth will come next. Now focus on your breathing. Notice how the more deeply you breathe, the more relaxed you become.

Formulate a question or desire in your mind. If it is a question, then let the words form clearly in your mind. If you wish, you may state them aloud. The more specific you make the question, the more clearly you will receive an answer. If it is a desire, then state it clearly and simply as though it has already been accomplished. Instead of "I want . . .," it is better to state "I have. . . ." Visualize the desired effect in as much detail as possible.

Now picture an opening. It might be a hole in the earth, a ladder, or simply a doorway. Picture an opening that works for you—a door that opens onto a stairwell, for example. Instead of a ladder, it could be the beginning of a flight of stairs, or of actual flight.

Soon you will meet a guide. Tell the guide your question or your desire. Follow your guide's lead or instruction. When you are finished, return by the same route. Remember to thank your guide and any other spirits that were involved.

Summary of the Basic Trance

1. Lie down and relax.

2. Focus on a question or desire.

3. Picture an opening and begin your journey.

4. When you meet your guide, tell the guide your question or desire.

5. Follow the guide's lead or instruction.

6. When finished, return by the same route.

7. Remember to thank the guide and other spirits.

Shapeshifting

After you have become familiar with the basic ritual, you will find it easier each time to quickly enter trance and begin your journey. Begin as you did in the basic ritual (page 67) by lying down and relaxing. As you relax, you may become aware of feelings of lightness and floating. When you are ready, allow yourself to step out of your body. This is similar to the experience you had with the basic ritual, but instead of entering a portal, your spirit will simply step away from the body and turn around.

Look at your body. See it in detail. Notice the rising and lowering caused by the quiet breathing. Just take a few minutes and familiarize yourself with the sensation of being outside and looking at yourself.

Now you may decide to make changes. Visualize them clearly. Superimpose the form you wish to have on your sleeping body. Then step into your body and feel the changes. Feel your body take on the form or the animal or person you visualized. When you are finished experiencing that form, you return to your own body the same way.

Ancient shamans would often use a costume to aid the process. For birds they would construct costumes of feathers. For wolves or bears they would wear cloaks or belts made or the skins of those animals. Such costumes are not necessary, but they can help with your focus. Effectiveness of this ritual (or any ritual) can also be enhanced by preceding it with the sauna, song, or dance.

Summary of Shapeshifting

1. Relax.
2. Step out of the body and turn around.
3. Decide to make changes. Visualize them.
4. Step into the body and be changed.
5. Feel the changes.
6. Return by the same method.
7. Enhance the ritual with costumes, song, or dance.

Visions and Dreams

As mentioned earlier, the purpose of rituals is to help the mage enter an alternate state of consciousness or trance. This trance is a fundamental tool of all magic.

We are all prisoners of our perceptions. We see only what we believe and we act on what we see. This should not be construed to imply that magic exists only in the imagination of the mage. On the contrary, a mage who changes into a bird *is* a bird. This can, and often does, mean that the mage's usual body stays behind, but the mage's spirit is elsewhere in the form of a bird. The mage can bring back information and even physical objects while in that form.

The reality is that once we change our perceptions, we are able to access power or principles that we are normally not aware of in our usual consciousness. This magical principle is not as unusual as it might at first sound. As a young man, I joined the Marine Corps. During our first few days, we were required to take a physical test that included a mile run. Few of us could complete the mile without walking. Within a few weeks, however, we found ourselves running five miles and further. Much of that transformation was a matter of perception. Similarly, examples could be given of people who had a critical perceptual change that allowed them to learn a foreign language or musical instrument. Are these examples any less magical for their commonness?

I have read that the aborigines in Australia can point out the exact location of the planet Venus anytime during the day. Modern westerners, of course, cannot do that; for us, the brightness of the sun makes Venus invisible. Their eyes are no different from ours—only their perceptions.

Trance is an effective tool to use in liberating ourselves from our own mundane perceptions. It is not surprising to find that trance plays a part in virtually every magical system. Other effective methods of inducing trance, or what we might call altered or magical states of consciousness, include fasting, sleep deprivation, various meditation techniques, dancing, drumming, and self-hypnosis.

The vision quest is also a fundamental technique of many ancient shamanistic societies, including the Native Americans and the Finns. Beginning with a sauna, the seeker would go off alone for several days with little or no food. This person's time would be spent in prayer, chanting, and performing ritual until the vision came. Since the mage is above all else pragmatic, the mage is free to explore various techniques and use those that are most effective. There is no obligation for the Finnish mage to adhere to some strict form or method—the more often the mage enters trance the easier trance becomes.

The Sacred Mushroom

Hallucinogenic mushrooms have been used by people throughout the world for religious and magical purposes. The mushroom of preference to the ancient Finns was the *Amanita muscaria*, or Fly Agaric. This is the traditional mushroom that is seen in so many pictures—red with white dots. It has a symbiotic relationship with the sacred birch tree and is used throughout northern

Eurasia. Other mushrooms may have similar effects; in North America, the most commonly used variety is the psilocybin mushroom.

To be used most effectively, these mushrooms should be used only with an experienced and knowledgeable mentor. They should never be used for recreation because they are sacred—an irreverent approach can offend the mushroom spirits. They should always be used in conjunction with a reverent ritual as an adjunct to the mage's seeking. The mentor can help the seeker to show the proper respect to the spirits and assist in the ritual and physical arrangements.

A mentor is also essential for safety. It is not wise to tamper with powerful spirits with whom you have little familiarity. There can be toxic reactions that result in severe illness or even death. A close relative to the *Amanita muscaria*, the *Amanita panthera*, for example is common in North America and is very toxic.

Despite these cautions, the sacred mushroom can play an important role in Finnish magic when used with reverence. In ancient times, it was particularly linked with shapeshifting and flying.

Sacrifice

Although it has always been an essential part of the practice of magic and of spiritual seeking, sacrifice is not well understood by modern western society. Even a brief examination of religious traditions reveals how universal the practice of sacrifice has been. The Old Testament tells how the ancients built altars of stone and offered a variety of sacrifices. The Mosaic law has very detailed instructions on the performance of sacrifices. The Christian tradition modified the practice by substituting a symbolic sacrifice in the form of bread and wine to remember the ultimate sacrifice of Christ. Similarly, we find that sacrifice played a central role in the worship of the ancient Greeks, Romans, Celts, and Germans.

Sacrifice serves several purposes. It is used to sanctify objects, occasions, and locations. This is done through the spiritual and symbolic influence of blood. Blood is, quite literally, the life of living things. It is sacred and should not be spilled lightly. For this reason, in sacrifice the animal should be killed quickly to avoid suffering. The mage does not hunt for pleasure—taking life is always a sacred act with far-reaching consequences.

Sacrifice is also used to invoke the influence of the gods. Certain animals are sacred to certain gods. In Nordic religion, the horse is sacred to Odin, the goat to Thor, the boar to Frey, and the sow to Freya. The sacrifice of these animals is used to honor and thank the gods.

Most importantly, sacrifice is a spiritual discipline. It is a reminder to the mage of the sacredness of life. It teaches detachment from worldly things and shows the willingness of the mage to do what is necessary in the pursuit of power and wisdom. It calls to mind the self-sacrifice of Odin as he hung pierced on Yggdrasill.

In practice, sacrifice is more like a sacred meal than a butchering. Prior to killing the animal, the gods should be invoked and the animal should be thanked for its gift. The animal must be killed quickly to avoid suffering. Blood from the animal is sprinkled to hallow the area or objects. Unusable portions of the animal can be burned; smoke is symbolic of messages to the gods. It is important, however, to use as much of the animal as possible. Skins can be used for clothing, drums, or other purposes. Bones can be used for making magical tools or decorations. The meat is prepared for eating. This sacred meal should, in most cases, be eaten by a group of worshippers—either a family or community. This is seen as symbolically eating the essence of the god. By participating in the sacrifice, all those involved become united with the god.

The Magic of Nature

The magic of the Finns is the magic of nature. The ancient Finns felt themselves to be fellow citizens in a universe inhabited by many other haltija. For the Finns, nature was not an obstacle to be overcome. Nor did they feel any responsibility for remaking nature into their own image. Nature for them was a source of life and healing. They lived close to nature and preferred their cabins in the forests to the congestion of great cities. For them, the best life was the life that was the closest to nature. Even those whose circumstances required them to live in cities found that their hearts were in the forests or on the rivers—and it is to the forests and rivers they returned at every opportunity.

Of course, there is evil—or at least opposition—in the fabric of nature, just as there is in human society. For the ancients, this was more a matter of problem solving than of morality. The problem was to determine who one was dealing with, and then to do what was needed to negotiate, persuade, or coerce a desired response. In dealing with nature, as in dealing with people, negotiation and persuasion are far more effective and less costly than coercion.

Learning from Nature

Then the Frost his songs recited,
And the rain its legends taught me;
Other songs the winds have wafted,
Or the ocean waves have drifted;
And their songs the birds have added,
And their magic spells the treetops.
—Kalevala[1]

The ancient Finns considered nature in general, and more specifically the various haltija, to be a primary source of magical knowledge. Finnish mages could understand the language of the birds. They sought to understand the true nature of all things. They spoke with the trees. The sought permission from Tapio for the hunt. They understood the benevolent spirits of plants, animals, and the forces of nature. But they also understood the malicious spirits such as Hiisi who is similar to Loki in Nordic mythology.

The eagle was a particular source of wisdom for the ancient Finns. The Kalevala tells of Väinämöinen being taught by the eagle. Ukko, the supreme god, is sometimes called Aïjä by the Finns and Aijo or Aije by the Lapps. Several scholars have noticed the similarity with Yakut Ai who is both creator and eagle. Aïjä, like Ai, is the ancestor of the shamans.

There are three primary ways of learning from nature: observation, reflection, and trance. Although these techniques must be applied separately, they are essentially three parts of a single process. This process is more than accumulating facts about healing plants and the cycles of nature. It is much more than classifying and naming. It is the process of understanding the reality of nature and of realizing one's own relationship with nature.

That is not to say that it is merely a mystical process, either. True magical knowledge combines understanding from both the material and the spiritual planes. For the true mage, one type of reality is no more real than the other. Both are essential to complete understanding, but also to complete application. The greatest mage of all time was noted not only for his skill as a singer, but also for his skill as a sailor or smith. The mage must be able to wield the axe or needle—or in our day, a computer or power tool—as well as the drum or the word.

Observation is a skill that one must acquire, and the best way to acquire it is through practice. There are obstacles to observation. The biggest obstacle is our preoccupation with other things. I read somewhere a story about the naturalist John Muir. He was in a city and saw some notable bird. He then noticed how no one else seemed to be aware of the bird or its song. As an experiment, he took some coins from his pocket and dropped them on the street. The result was that all those around him turned to look at the money. We notice what we are interested in.

Preoccupation can interfere with observation in other ways as well. We tend to see what we expect to see. To a great extent, our definition of the world determines the nature of the world. That is one of the reasons many in the western world fail to notice the magic that surrounds them. They have defined the world as a place of Newtonian cause and effect with no place for the magical. Even when confronted with evidence to the contrary, they disregard it as illusion or delusion. In other words, many people fail to see what is in the world because they suppose that they already *know* what is there.

Observation begins with curiosity. The attitude to adopt is that of a child. Allow yourself to be impressed with the newness of things. Remember what it was like as a child to sit and stare at the delicate crystalline structure of a dandelion in seed. That feeling was literally en-joy-ment. When we allow ourselves to view the world as it really is, then we experience joy. Most adults in the western world cannot feel that joy for dandelions because they do not see the plant for what it is, but for what they have defined it as being—a weed. Be curious. Look at the world for the first time every time and you will experience joy. And that joy will make the act of observation compelling.

Begin your observation with little things, like flowers and leaves. Then move on to larger things, such as trees and landscapes. Do not attempt to memorize or analyze. Just observe. Watch and notice how the world changes with changes in light and seasons. Enjoy noticing small details such as colors and lines. Notice the total picture. Notice the movements of animals and birds as well as their appearance.

Look for patterns as well as details. These patterns have magical significance. They were included in the creation of things as a means of conveying meaning.

> *Now the isles were formed already,*
> *In the sea the rocks were planted;*
> *Pillars of the sky established,*
> *Lands and continents created;*
> *Rocks engraved as though with figures*
> —Kalevala[2]

This last line could be translated as patterns cut upon the rocks. Patterns, or in Finnish *kirja,* are symbols of magic. They can be either man-made—as with runes—or natural. Those who learn to read them have access to a library of secret lore.

As you progress in your ability as an observer, you will be able to expand your observation to other senses. Lay outside and observe with your ears. Hear the movement of nature. Listen for the details and the pattern. Take off your shoes and observe with your feet—feel the texture of rocks, wood, and earth underfoot. Be aware of smells of grass, trees, and air. Notice how smells change, just as sights change, with seasons and time.

Practice observation at night as well as in the daytime. Observe with your eyes, ears, nose, and skin. Notice how smells change, just as sights change, with seasons and time.

Make observation a habit. This will benefit you in each area of your life. It will improve your ability to communicate with others. It will make you a more careful worker. It will enhance your enjoyment of life. As you continue the practice of observation, you will see the connections of things.

Observation alone is little more than awareness and storing information. This information is processed through pondering and reflection. To be a mage is to be true to one's humanness. For some of nature's children, it is enough to observe. For them, awareness alone makes knowledge usable. That is not the case with humans. We must add understanding to awareness. We must think to fulfill our nature as humans.

To ponder is to think. Consider the things you see and order them in your mind. Ask about the meaning of your observations. Trace the chain of events that led to certain observances. This is the practice of the skilled hunter who tracks his prey through the clues left in the earth. This is also the practice of the singer who creates a story to explain the true nature of things. This is also the skill of the craftsman who learns to apply the qualities of things to create new things. This is the way of the mage.

> *So he pondered and reflected*
> *How to find the words he needed,*
> *And obtain the spells of magic,*
> *From among the brains of swallows,*
> *From the heads of flocks of wild swans,*
> *From the shoulders of the goose-flocks,*
> *Then he went the words to gather...*
> *So he pondered and reflected*
>
> —Kalevala[3]

In a very real sense, the process of thinking is the process of creation. Our thoughts, our definitions, our understandings of the world determine our interactions with the world. In other words, we create our own world from our limited observations and thoughts. We must be careful, therefore, not to mistake our thoughts for the ultimate truth. If we make that mistake, observations will cease. Those who believe that they know the ultimate truth have no need to learn. The process of pondering and reflection must be a creative process of constant revision. We must be willing to sacrifice our pet theories and understandings just as a potter sacrifices flawed pots in order to make better pots. Perhaps a better analogy would be the farmer who willingly harvests and then plows up a field in order to plant again and harvest again. The process of thinking is continuous and creative, or else it becomes stagnant and nonproductive.

But learning from nature does not stop with observation and thought. Magical learning requires trance work. It requires the mage to enter an altered state of consciousness in order to become aware of things beyond the material plane. If you have already practiced observing, or have even thought of the process, then you have probably experienced changes in your vision. You may have noticed that your awareness of time was distorted. An hour spent looking at nature might have seemed "spaced out" while you were pondering the things you had seen. You were in a trance—or at least the beginning of a trance. During these periods, great insights can seem to flow from your unconscious. These are times of the greatest creativity and intuition.

There are many paths to trance. You may choose to follow your observations and thoughts with a shamanic journey. In such a journey, there might be a specific type of knowledge or power you seek. Begin with preparatory drumming and enter your journey with chanting. You will enter a different world—a world that is just as real as this material plane—and each journey will teach you more.

You may choose to simply sing or chant to do your trance. You will find that as you increase your ability to enter quickly into trance, you will find words given to you. These new songs will be power songs to you.

The actual method you choose to enter trance is not as important as the trance itself. You may choose to meditate or use self-hypnosis. The important thing is that you regularly allow yourself to experience an altered state of consciousness. This, too, is a skill that requires practice. The more skilled you become, the more aware you will become of intuitions and non-ordinary states of reality. This will enhance your singing and your rituals as well.

Spirits and gods are not perceptible in ordinary states of reality. They exist on a different plane and must be perceived differently from things on the everyday plane of existence. That is not to say that they are not real. Atoms are the building blocks of the physical world, but atoms are not perceptible through normal vision. They are real. The light spectrum contains wavelengths that are not perceptible to human eyes and there are sounds that are beyond human ears. Reality is not limited to our normal sensory input. When we enter trance, we become sensitive to a reality that is normally outside our sensations. The more familiar we become with trance, the more easily we will be able to observe and interact with that realm.

Among the things we learn in an altered state of consciousness is that not all things on the spiritual plane are of equal value. There are gods, but there are also lesser spirits that have little power or knowledge. They can be very persistent in their attempts to get our attention, but as we become familiar with the spiritual realm, we will learn to differentiate between lesser and greater things.

In trance work we learn the true nature of things, including spirits. Spirits do not necessarily have human form, or even personalities as such, but it is useful to imagine them as people in order to understand them. That is the reason the ancient mages gave names to the spirits that inhabit everything. The names give us a method for ordering and using our knowledge.

Some of the most important learning from nature comes when least expected. Certainly observation, pondering, and trance are essential, but it seems that as our skills develop, nature offers her gifts freely and spontaneously. You will find intuitions flowing freely into your mind. You may find yourself visited unexpectedly by some spirit. If you pay attention to the unexpected intuitions, you will find that they will increase in frequency and significance.

Finding Sacred Places

There are sacred places, places where access to the spirits is easier than in other places. Many of these places have become the focus of formal religious activities and sites for the erection of temples and churches. It is interesting to note how many of the churches in Europe are built on the ruins of pagan temples, and how those temples were built on the ruins of temples before them.

Often, we find these sacred places in nature. There, too, we find that people have used them as meeting places or places of worship: Mount Shasta, Stonehenge, Mount Sinai. There are smaller places as well that are often known to local people or noticed by those who are sensitive to spiritual things. Bodies of water are frequently sites of power. For the ancient Finns, there were sacred rivers and lakes—*pyhajoki* and *pyhajarvi*. There were bottomless lakes that were considered to be entrances to the kingdom of the water god, Nakki.

Such sacred places enhance your magical abilities and energize your emotions and thoughts. The larger sacred places that have been used for spiritual seeking are enhanced by the collective spirit of the people and so are made even more powerful. Likewise, negativity and destructive behavior can infect a location. It is best to avoid tainted negative places. It is also wise to prepare yourself before knowingly entering a sacred place.

In any area there are both sacred places and negative places. You may already be aware of some of them. There may be a special place where you enjoy going to sit and think. There may be another place that you always carefully avoid. Most likely, you are responding intuitively to the spirits of these places.

You can locate these sacred places simply by following your intuitions. Sit down and close your eyes. Get a sense of your surroundings and the spirits around you. Seek the guidance of the spirits in finding a sacred place. Now walk with your eyes closed until your feelings tell you that you have found the place. You will be able to feel the energy there. You will be aware of the presence of the spirits. Once there, sit quietly and immerse yourself in the sacredness of the setting. Study the rocks, plants, and elements. Attend to their shapes, textures, and colors. Notice their subtle changes during the course of the day. It is a quiet but very direct procedure.

Once you have found the place, go there often to meditate and to do trance work. Enhance the place with your thoughts. Avoid bringing evil, negative thoughts into the place, just as you would avoid tracking mud onto a white carpet. The ancients used to dedicate such places and fence them off to indicate their sacredness. Perhaps you will be able to create such an outdoor temple.

Although such places are most effective in the outdoors, it is also possible to find sacred places in your own yard and home. If you wish to create a shrine in your backyard, follow your intuitions and seek the help of the spirits in finding the right place. Once you have the place, treat it as you would a shrine. Take the time to center and calm yourself before going there. Use it for meditation, rituals, and singing sacred songs. Follow your intuition on how to create your sacred space. You might wish to build an altar of wood or stone. Such an altar ought to be at least two feet by two feet. You may choose to consecrate lesser sites by placing a sacred stone, a *sejda,* as a talisman. If you wish, you can plant a tree on that sacred place and create your own sacred garden.

In former days, many Finnish families had a lucky family tree. This tree would often be fenced to indicate its sacredness. An alternative to the sacred tree is to cut a ladder into or attach a ladder to a tree to create a sacred tree for use in ritual work. The ancients designated certain groves as sacred and performed their rituals around a central tree, which represented the great World Tree—the center of the world. It is the tree that gives life. Its roots are in the lower world. Its trunk is in this world and its branches reach to the upper world. But that tree in the grove was only a symbol. The World Tree, the Axis of the World, is everywhere. Everywhere is the center of creation. Every time is both eternal and now. You stand at the intersection of the material and spiritual planes and only your awareness hinders your ability to move and function well in either plane. The important thing is to be aware of the sacredness around you, and then to use those sacred places to enhance your own power.

Controlling Nature

In the Kalevala we can read how Väinämöinen landed in a treeless country and planted trees. He employed the spirit of agriculture, Sampsa Pellervoinen, to plant pines, spruces, heather, birches, alders, cherries, willows, rowans, junipers, and oaks. As the trees prospered, birds came, perched in the branches, and sang. Other plants also flourished because of Väinämöinen's labor. He was instructed in his labor by birds who explained the way to grow oats, so he cleared the trees to prepare the ground for oats. But he left one great tree standing.

> *In the sky there soared an eagle,*
> *Of the birds of air the greatest,*
> *And he came and gazed around him:*
> *"Wherefore is the work unfinished,*
> *And the birch-tree still unfallen?*
> *Wherefore spare the beauteous birch-tree?"*

> *Said the aged Väinämöinen,*
> *"Therefore is the birch left standing,*
> *That the birds may perch upon it;*
> *And the birds of air may rest there."*
> —Kalevala[4]

That is the way of Finnish magic. Humans must do things to control and modify nature. It is the nature of humans. We plant seeds and grow crops. We take from the trees and the earth resources to make our tools and shelter. We even take from the animals for food and clothing. But in all this, we show reverence to nature and seek the aid of the spirits. The Finnish mage controls changes by first becoming aware of change. This awareness also increases the mage's sense of responsibility.

At times we struggle with nature. We fight off the life forms that cause illness. We take action against vermin and pests. We do what we can to fend off the ravages of floods and storms. In our struggle, we are aided by charms and magical power as well as practical skill. But through it all, we honor nature and seek to live in peace with all creatures. Through it all we seek to do only good.

We do not seek to make nature over again in our image. We seek to use our influence for the benefit of all. The way of Finnish magic is the way of balance and ecology. It is the way of harmony and environmentalism. The mage does not seek power in order to control others or nature. The mage seeks power in order to benefit the universe.

Summary

By combining the magical techniques and principles enumerated in this chapter, you will find that your attunement to nature increases. Take time to observe nature, to learn to accept nature with all of your senses, and make this an habitual practice.

Learning from Nature

1. Practice observing. Look for patterns as well as details. Remember that naturally occurring patterns, or *kirja,* are magical symbols. Become aware of changes. The ability to control change (i.e., magic) begins with an awareness of change.

2. Learn to observe with all your senses. Reacquaint yourself with the textures, sounds, and smells of nature.

3. Make the practice of observation habitual to increase your awareness. By increasing your awareness, you will develop your intuition. You will also increase your sense of responsibility toward the rest of nature.

4. Enter trance and continue your learning.

5. Attend to your intuitions when not in trance.

6. Enjoy nature. There is more magical learning in the wonderment of watching a soaring hawk or blowing apart the crystalline structure of a dandelion than there is in all the texts you will ever read.

Endnotes

1. *Kalevala: The Land of the Heroes*, 3.
2. Ibid, 8.
3. Ibid, 188.
4. Ibid, 18.

THE MAGIC OF SONG

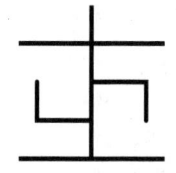

We are all well-acquainted with the magic of song; we have all been inspired by song, moved to tears or to smiles. Music can stir men to acts of courage. Music is used by religions to create a feeling of sacredness. The prophets of Aphrodite at Paphos spoke to the music of harps. The prophet Elisha called for a minstrel to play to assist him in finding water for the armies of Judah and Ephraim. We read in the Bible of a band of ancient prophets who came down from a high place with psaltery, timbrel, pipe, and harp prophesying as they went. Music has been used to enchant and to inspire. Its very name recalls goddesses of the ancient world.

Music is a powerful tool in the creation and use of emotion—emotion is a powerful magical tool. It should be no surprise, then, to find that music has been used in many magical traditions. The sirens sang sailors to their doom. The ancient Egyptians believed in the magic of music. Music itself seems to have a magical quality. This is due in part to the nature of the universe, which in a very real sense is composed of vibrations. Changes in these vibrations can result in transformations of one thing into another. Changes in the vibrations can also alter the quality of things in such a way as to allow actions that are normally impossible. Music also facilitates entering trance, and during these altered states of consciousness it seems that the wavelength of the mind is changed, which again allows actions that would normally be impossible.

The use of music is especially important to the magic of the Finns, which grows out of the ecstatic techniques of shamanism. It is so central that in the Kalevala, the word "singing" is synonymous with magic.

For those interested, there are recordings available of Finnish shaman chants and the songs of the Kalevala. There are also commercial recordings of folk songs and folk-influenced music that are useful to anyone who wants to follow the Finnish path of magic. Notable among these are the recordings of Värttina, a group of ten musicians who sing folk music with a strong Karelian influence that includes rune song lyrics.

The music of Seppo "Paroni" Paakkunainen, a Finnish flautist, is also notable. He plays the *tuohi huilu*, a birchbark flute wrapped in strips of bark. It is high pitched and sometimes also known as *paimen huilu*, a cowherd's flute.

Of course, there is the music of Jean Sibelius. Although not "folk," his compositions are strongly influenced by the Kalevala. Anyone who is seriously interested in getting closer to the tradition should consider listening to his music, including *Finlandia* and *Swan of Tuonela*, works he based directly upon the Kalevala.

Shaman Songs

Shamanism in its classical form involves the use of music and dance to achieve an altered state of consciousness. Native American shamanism has become familiar to many through the writings of Carlos Castaneda, Michael Harner, and others. But the term *shaman* comes from Siberia, and shamans can still be found throughout Asia.

Shamanism is not strictly confined to primitive, non-industrialized societies—shamanism can be found throughout the world. It is widely practiced in Korea, where the *mudang* is called in to perform healings, and even public dedications. Shamanism was also a major influence on the development of more formalized religions such as Lamaism and Taoism. The magic of the

Finns, like their language, also originated in Asia and has much in common with its Asian counterparts.

The shaman functions as a healer, an intermediary with the spirits, and a psychopomp or guide for the spirits of the dead. The shaman typically enters trance through the use of the rhythmic music and dance. During the trance, the shaman communicates with the spirits, often going on a voyage to the Under world to gain needed knowledge and power to help others. The application of that knowledge and power might be through a healing ceremony, a song, or other ritual.

Any monotonous repeated activity can be used to induce a trance. In fact, trances are an everyday occurrence. Most of us have had the experience of driving a car from point A to point B only to arrive at point B without remembering doing all the turning, shifting, braking, and steering needed to get there. In this case, we have had experienced a spontaneous trance state brought on by the monotony of the drive.

Repetition and rhythm also aid in trance induction. Most of us have experienced the reverie that occurs when we are overcome by a fine symphony or other musical piece. Repetition and rhythm are also factors in the so-called "runner's high." Dancing, too, can be used to induce trance. It is no wonder that the shaman uses music and dance to enter "God's hour" as the Finnish mages refer to trance.

The Shaman's Drum

The traditional drum was made of pine root and covered with an ox skin or buckskin. A piece of wood was placed underneath as a handle. It was similar to the Irish *bodhrann*—a wooden hoop with a tight animal hide stretched over it and held in place with brass tacks. The shamans would hang the hooves of various animals around the drum. The drums were adorned with painted decorations, which frequently included nine lines, as well as the emblems of gods, the sun, the moon, and animals that could bring luck or harm to animals. The drumstick was a horn hammer lined with beaver skin.

When divining, the shamans of old would place pieces of copper or wings of a copper-colored bird on the drum. They would then beat the drum and the objects would hop until they landed on a line. This would be an indicator for the diviner.

Although it is not necessary to have a traditional shaman's drum, the closer one can come to that model the better. Any traditional Native American drum will do. As with most magical instruments it is better, when possible, to make the tool yourself. Books containing instructions for making Native American drums are available in most libraries.

Whether you buy or build a drum, you should decorate it yourself with line drawings to represent the spirits that are most important to you. These might include pictures of great shamans or gods such as Väinämöinen or Ilmarinen. In addition to drums, the Finnish shaman also uses rattles, click sticks, and chanting to set a steady regular beat.

A ceremony usually begins with drumming, rattles, and click sticks setting a steady regular beat. This might take place for ten minutes or more. Soon, the shaman and participants begin to notice a shift in their consciousness as the rhythm begins to have its effect. As the consciousness begins to shift, the music changes to single drumming. This single drumming is slightly faster in tempo and seems to draw the shaman into the rhythm like a leaf entering an eddy in a stream. As the shaman continues into the trance and begins the voyage to the Under world, the drumming stops and the chanting begins.

The chanting, like the drumming, is repetitious and rhythmic. It usually consists of nonsense syllables sung in couplets.

> *Hey yo, hey yo, hey yah-ah*
> *Hey yo, hey yo, hey yo*
> *Hey yo, hey yo, hey yah-ah*
> *Hey yo, hey yo, hey yo*

The pattern is repeated continuously as long as the journey continues. It ceases only when the shaman returns to normal consciousness.

The drumming and the chanting help the shaman shut out distractions and focus on the journey. As the drumming and chanting continue, all participants begin to experience trance. Their breathing becomes deeper and more regular. Their muscles relax and their perceptions begin to change. The shamanic trance can be so deep that at times they can appear to be in a coma. During these trances, the shaman may journey to the underworld to gain knowledge or may travel astrally to great distances. During these trance states, it is also possible for the shaman to change to an animal or bird. Wolves, bears, and reindeer are animal forms commonly chosen by the ancients.

A variant on this is to add to the drumming. The dance can be line dancing, ring dancing, or an individual dance, but is always rather simple, repetitive, and rhythmic. Individual dances often imitate the movements of a totem or power animal that has special significance as a guide or helper. The bodily rhythm has the same effect as the music and seems particularly useful when invoking spirits. During an invocation, the shaman acts as a medium and the spirit communicates through the body of the shaman. This is not to be confused with evocation, which is when the mage calls forth spirits to communicate with them.

The informed reader will notice that this sounds very similar to the ceremonies of the American Indians. And indeed it should. Shamanism whether practiced by the Navajo, the Korean, the Irkutsk, or the Finn is essentially the same. There may be variants in costume, structure of instruments, or other manifestation, but the basic structure and purpose is the same.

Singing as Magic

The magic of the Kalevala is usually expressed in singing. Through singing, shamans are able to heal illness and transform the world. Singing, just like the instrumental music of the shaman, can be used to induce trance to gain knowledge and power or to induce trance to gain the emotional power and will of the mage. Singing is used to help bring the singer and the hearer into an awareness of the spiritual realm.

Singing, unlike shaman songs, places great importance on the words. Everything has a name and an origin. If you can discover the origin of a thing, then you can have power over it. "Origin" is not to be understood in the sense of physical beginnings, but rather it should be understood in terms of "true nature." If we know the origins of something, then we understand its true nature and its connection with everything else in the world. For this reason, many origin songs take on a mythic quality. The purpose is not to explain origin, but rather to demonstrate to the thing and to the singer that the thing and its true nature is understood.

The words of the song then can be passed down from ancient times with the traditions preserved in the Kalevala. These represent a common core of knowledge for all singers of magic, a beginning place. The words might be found in other sources as well: Hebrew words from Kabbalah or the scriptures, Enochian words, words of hymns, words of folk songs, poetry, words from other traditions. The source is not as important as the vitality and the reality of the word for the singer.

The words must express the singer's feelings and connect the singer with the reality of the thing being sung.

Important sources for words are the spirits themselves. The spirits of nature are the best instructors of the true nature of the things of nature. The spirits of ancestors are sources of comfort and wisdom. In trance, it is possible to recover power words from the world of spirits and to be instructed directly by the spirit of an ancestor or a great mage from the other side. This is what Väinämöinen did—he went first to the land of the dead but did not find the power he needed. He then sought instruction directly from the mouth of the great wizard Antero Vipunen.

> *Väinämöinen old and steadfast,*
> *Had not found the words he wanted*
> *In the dark abode of Tuoni,*
> *In the eternal realms of Mana,*
> *And for evermore he pondered,*
> *In his head reflected ever,*
> *Where the words he might discover,*
> *And obtain the charms he needed.*
>
> *Vipunen, in songs so famous,*
> *He the sage so old in wisdom,*
> *In whose mouth was mighty magic,*
> *Power unbounded in his bosom,*
> *Opened then his mouth of wisdom,*
> *Of his spells the casket opened,*
> *Sang his mighty spells of magic,*
> *Chanted forth of all the greatest,*
> *Magic songs of the Creation,*
> *From the very earliest ages*
>
> —Kalevala[1]

But the words of magic songs are not set in stone. The singer is free to invent new songs. The critical part of song construction is that the words and the songs themselves are true to the singers' emotions and true to the nature of the thing being sung. Done with the real intent, the song can then effect changes in the world by becoming the vehicle of the singer's will. These changes begin on the spiritual plane, but will eventually manifest on the material plane as well.

The best way to discover a song or to receive one from the spirits is to seek it in nature. Seek out a remote area. Fast or eat sparingly during your search. Do not follow any set plan. Just wander where your feelings and the spirit lead you. At times you may walk, at other times you may feel like sitting. As the day goes on, you will become aware first of the melody and then the words for the song.

An important function of songs is the evocation of spirits. This is best done by visualizing and personalizing the spirit you wish to evoke. Remember, everything has a spirit, so be specific. It is not enough to evoke some general "spirit of weather" if you are concerned about the tomatoes in your garden. The names of many spirits can be found in this book, but a complete list would be essentially a list of everything that is. It is not necessary to confine yourself to Finnish names; spirits are not particularly Finnish and in fact the ancient Finns borrowed names from other cultures. Use names that feel appropriate for you. If you are in the Southwest Desert, perhaps Spanish, Navajo, or Hopi names will feel more appropriate. In Louisiana, you might prefer French. Use names that feel right and real to you. Experiment with several names, try out words from Hebrew and Enochian. You may find that some spirits have more than one name, and on occasion you might use one name, but at other times prefer another. The name should make it easy for you to visualize the spirit.

Evocation and communication with the spirits is central to Finnish magic. The mage must evoke spirits frequently—during rituals, with charms, in song. Evocation leads to familiarity with the spirits and the spirits bring knowledge and power. This is not to be done lightly, however. Evocation brings the spirits. Simply stating the name of the spirit or calling upon the nature of the spirit will cause the spirit to attend. Spirits, after all, are not so different from humans. If I call your name, within your hearing, I will get your attention. You could even be preoccupied with other activities, but the sound of your name will cause you to listen. This is true for spirits as well. Call on them and you will get their attention. This fact is reflected in the folk sayings of many cultures. The English folk saying "speak of the devil" and the Korean *sokdam* "the tiger too comes when I speak" both reflect this truth. The demons and spirits come to listen when their names are spoken. How would you feel if someone were to call you, but not really wish to speak? Or what if they called you to mock you? You would probably be angry, and so it is with the spirits. Do not call them lightly. Even when you are not aware of their presence, they are there.

Developing your sensitivity increases your awareness of the spirits, it does not create them.

Because singing, as all magic, is an exercise of will, it is enhanced in a group of people whose wills are united. One method for uniting the will of a group through song is for a single singer to begin the singing. This sets the stage and prepares the singer and the audience to enter into a trance state. When the singer begins to enter the trance, he or she stops singing and the audience takes over. This continues until the singer returns from the trance. In certain areas of Finland, the singing is done by groups of women who dance as they sing. The classic method of singing used by the Kalevala bards was for two men to join hands and sing. The main singer would sing and the supporting singer would respond as they composed anew the ancient songs while rocking back and forth to the music.

> *Let us clasp our hands together,*
> *Let us interlock our fingers;*
> *Let us sing a cheerful measure,*
> *Let us use our best endeavors,*
> *While our dear ones hearken to us,*
> *And our loved ones are instructed,*
> *While the young are standing round us,*
> *Of the rising generation,*
> *Let them learn the words of magic,*
> *And recall our songs and legends,*
> *Of the belt of Väinämöinen,*
> *Of the forge of Ilmarinen*
>
> —Kalevala[2]

These songs were often sung to the accompaniment of the kantele. The kantele is a five-stringed instrument that is held on the knees and plucked with the fingers. It is more of a zither, although it is usually called a harp in English.

The songs are usually sung aloud and in groups with great feeling. They can also be sung in solitude. They need not even be sung loudly. They can even be sung under the breath. If the will is sufficiently developed, they might not need to be sung at all. The intent, understanding, and emotion are the essential factors. The song is but a vehicle or tool to focus the will.

> *If no other bard comes forward*
> *To accompany my singing,*
> *Then alone my songs I'll carol,*
> *And will now commence my singing,*
> *For to sing was I created*
>
> —Kalevala[3]

Singing to Heal

When singing to heal, the singer sings of the origin of the thing that caused the injury or illness. Next, appropriate curative steps are taken such as administering medicine, herbs, poultices, and lotions. The next step is to request the assistance of a spirit; an appropriate middle level spirit is usually evoked and asked to help with the healing. If the healing process needs further aid, then more and higher spirits can be called upon including Jumala himself.

The idea of singing the origins demonstrates to the patient and to the injury that the singer has sufficient power to bring about the healing. This sets up an expectation of healing within the patient that aids the natural and magical processes. Research shows that, even in modern medical procedures, the placebo effect plays a major role in the process of healing. That is simply to say that belief is a powerful curative.

It is important to provide the patient with appropriate symbols that provide a focus for the process of healing. These symbols are sometimes material, but can simply be vivid word pictures created through the songs. In other words, it is not necessary to sing of germs and viruses—in fact, such pictures are probably too hard to visualize and too "unreal" to our mental conception. It is better to create meaningful concrete images that can be held by the mind and targeted by the will and the emotions. The singer must visualize the desired outcome as the song is sung. The focus of the will and emotions together in the trance state bring about a change in the spiritual plane. Spiritual change always precedes change in the material plane.

Finnish Charms

Charms are the simplest forms of songs. Traditionally, they accompany almost every activity from cleaning a floor to building a house. They incorporate all the elements of singing magic and one should not be deceived by their simplicity. When used by one who has practiced developing their will through frequent trance work and magical singing, they can be powerful tools. Following are some examples of traditional charms.

For a Bruised or Scratched Hand

Hyi! From what place is distress?
Is it from an old hag?
Or from the raspberry bushes?
Or from the fence post?
Where the raven turns black
The black bird is created - Hyi!

Hyi! Mista on puuttunu?
Vaikka vanhoista akkoista?
Vaikka vattu ranniaista?
Vaikka saipaan sijasta?
Jost'an korppi korvettu
Musta lintu muokatta—Hyi!

To Prevent Frozen Fingers

Cold, son of the wind.
Don't chill my fingertips
Don't freeze my hands;
Freeze the water willows
Chill the birch chunks

Pakkanen puhirin poika
Alakylmaa kynsiain'
Ala kynsiain' palele;
Palele ves' pajuja,
Kylma koivun konkaleita.

Controlling Hiccups

This charm to cure hiccups is an exercise in breath control. It must be said without taking a second breath.

> *Hiccup to the heddle*
> *Second to the bark*
> *Third to the birch*
> *Fourth to the needle*
> *Fifth to the thicket*
> *Sixth to the spruce*
> *Seventh to the pole*
> *Eighth to the stump*
> *Ninth up*
> *Tenth to the neighbor*

> *Nikko niineen*
> *Toinen tuoheen*
> *Kolmas koivun*
> *Neljas neulaan*
> *Viides viitaan*
> *Kuudes kuuseen*
> *Seitsemas seipaaseen*
> *Kahdeksas kantoon*
> *Yhdeksas yllaa*
> *Kymenes kyllaa*

The three traditional charms above are not only examples of charms, but are notable as examples of how the Finns brought their traditions with them to America. These charms were all collected in Minnesota from Finnish-Americans.[4] The Kalevala, of course, contains many examples of charms—about sixty-five. They include the exotic, such as charms on the origin of the water dragon, and a charm for ski equipment. But they also include the very practical—such as charms for stanching blood, charms of protection from disease and to restrain injuries, charms for a woman in labor, and charms for summoning help. There are charms that specifically apply to magic, such as exorcism charms, protective charms against wizards, warrior's charms, healer's charms, lot-casting charms, charms to control the winds, charms to gain God's support, and more.

These charms are often many lines in length and are not to be confused with the simple charms that are sometimes passed down in folklore. They are powerful when sung by those with power. That is not to say that there is not power in the simpler charms themselves. The power is not in the words alone but in the understanding, will, and feeling of the singer.

When studying the songs of magic, it is important to remember that their purpose is not merely to effect changes in the spiritual existence of the singer. The goal of Finnish magic is to bring about an awareness and reverence of the spiritual that is a thread running through the fabric of creation. Of course, that awareness and reverence will bring with it power, but to the true mage, power is not an end unto itself. More important than the power to control the wind and shape the world is the power to help others and the ability to live in harmony and peace with one's neighbors, family, and self.

Endnote

1. *Kalevala: The Land of Heroes,* 196 and 210.
2. Ibid, 2.
3. Ibid, 272.
4. T. P. Coffin and H. Cohen. *Folklore in America* (Garden City, NY: Doubleday and Co., 1996) 103–105.

The Sauna

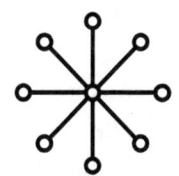

Perhaps nothing is so Finnish as the sauna. It is much more than a steam bath. It is a place of refuge from the outside world. It is a place of cleanliness and peace, of healing and togetherness. When the Finns moved to a new area, the first building they would erect was the sauna and they would live there while building their larger house. No Finnish homestead was complete without one—or sometimes two saunas. This practice was continued in the colony of New Sweden and was yet another way in which the Finns found themselves similar to their Native American neighbors. The practice of the sauna among the Finns is similar in both purpose and practice to the Native American sweat lodge. The practice among the earliest New World Finns died out with the other vestiges of Finnish culture as the English and the other western Europeans became increasingly dominant—both politically and socially. The western Europeans did not consider cleanliness in general, or bathing in particular, to be especially desirable.

Later in the eighteenth century, Finnish immigrants to America built saunas in the midwest and the northwest. And in this century, the sauna has become familiar to most Americans, although certainly not to the extent that it is to the Finns.

The typical sauna experience consists of exposure to the intense heat of the steam-heated sauna. While sitting in the sauna, the Finns use birch whisks to lightly beat themselves to stimulate circulation. After sitting in the sauna for as long as possible, some will leave to cool themselves in a snow bank or a cold stream.

The sauna is a quiet, serious experience. It is not somber, but it is not a place for loud laughter or boisterous behavior. It is both private and public. While it is a wonderful place to sit and meditate, it can be disconcerting to the westerner because of the nudity. In the old Finnish tradition, entire families would sit together in the sauna. If there were visitors, they would be equally

The Sauna

welcomed. The westerner who has been taught that the body is a thing of shame may find this a little uncomfortable. The overly sexualized westerner who has come to believe that the nudity of the opposite sex is a thing to be either shunned or leered at will find that the intense heat of the sauna makes activities other than breathing very difficult to think about.

In addition to cleanliness and relaxation, the sauna offers healing and at times has literally saved lives. Often it has served as a hospital, and in former times it was a better hospital than those available in most places. It was accessible because every family had one and it was exceptionally clean from the steam, heat, water, and soap. There in the clean warmth of the sauna the patient could find relaxation. The sauna was also an ideal place for giving birth—many Finns were literally born in a sauna.

Finns can be almost fanatical when espousing the virtues of the sauna. They will use the sauna for curing almost every conceivable illness including sunburn, fevers, gout, rheumatism, infections, arthritis, insomnia, even a broken heart. This might sound like superstition to westerners, but sauna therapy does seem to work. People with colds enter the sauna sniffling and emerge clear-headed, pain from sunburns and arthritis is relieved. Such cures are common.

As with everything, the sauna has a spirit. The haltija of the sauna knows and feels. It is the spirit of the sauna that purifies, heals, and consecrates. If offended, the spirit punishes just as easily as it heals. For this reason it is important to respect the sauna.

The sauna, much like the sweat lodge of the Native Americans, provides a path to altered states of consciousness and visions. Like the sweat lodge, the sauna provides a needed purification prior to rituals for those who are seeking power and knowledge on the spiritual plane—it is not just to clean, but also to consecrate. In the sauna, the four elements of the universe are brought together in one place; earth, fire, air, and water combine to create a place of power and healing—a sacred place.

The heat of the sauna is conducive to trance. After sitting in a very hot sauna for just a little while, you may begin to feel light-headed and even giddy. This can be the first step to trance. Additionally, the sauna is very relaxing, a quality desirable to those who are attempting trance work.

Preparing the Sauna

Saunas are traditionally made of logs. It is possible to find commercial sauna builders in America today, but if you do not have access to a commercial sauna or you would like to build one of your own, it should be constructed of logs on the pattern of a small log cabin. In lieu of a log sauna, it is possible to build a sauna in the style of a Native American structure, or you may use a tent.

The next essential ingredient is the sauna heater or *kiaus*. The sauna can be heated either by wood or electricity, usually to a temperature of 180° F (80° C) to 200° F (95° C) or more.

The vapor, or *löyly*, is created by throwing water on sizzling hot rocks or directly on the top of the stove. Thus, the so-called dry sauna is not appropriate for this type of magical work.

The *vihtas* are traditionally birch whisks soaked in hot water prior to use. During the sauna, they are used to softly beat the skin all over the body. This massages, stimulates circulation, and creates a fresh fragrance in the sauna. It is possible to substitute cedar or oak whisks. Simply cut a length that is manageable for a whisk and soak it in hot water prior to use just as with the birch whisks.

Finally, there should be a source of cold water easily accessible for cooling down after the sauna. This can be a natural source such as a stream or lake or it can be a shower or swimming pool.

Summary of Elements of the Sauna

1. The Sauna itself. Either a small cabin, a commercially built sauna, or a Native American style steam lodge.
2. A sauna heater, also known as a kiaus.
3. Bucket and dipper for throwing water on the heater to create löyly (vapor).
4. Vihtas, traditional birch whisks (oak or cedar can be substituted). Soak these in hot water prior to use.

Taking a Sauna

Enter the sauna as you would enter a sacred place. Shed your clothes as you shed the world and the things of the world. Clear your mind of mundane things so that as your body is cleansed of impurities, so too your mind might be cleaned. Concern yourself only with the feel of the heat, the sensations on your skin, and the here-and-now of breathing and moving.

When you leave the sauna, go immediately to a cold shower or—as like the old Finns—to a snowbank or cold stream. You will find the cold surprisingly refreshing, instead of painful, after the heat of the sauna.

Now you are clean, purified, invigorated, and ready to listen to the shaman's drums and sing the mage's songs. But there is power in the sauna alone. The mental and physical experience of the sauna brings the mage in touch with self and in harmony with creation. Väinämöinen used the sauna as a tool to drive away a pestilence.

Sacred Times

The ancient Finns recognized the significance of the seasons and the inherent power associated with certain times of the year. Chief among the seasonal festivals were the celebration of the equinox, solstice, new moon, full moon, midsummer, and ancestral dates. The solstices and equinoxes were usually connected with the Earth Mother. In addition to the seasonal festivals, the mage could recognize any number of daily or weekly personal sacred times.

Festivals

Festivals are times of community celebration and empowerment. They are in a very real sense "sacred parties." Most of the major festivals center on changes in the seasons. They are celebrations of life and change, but also times for respecting and invoking the powers of nature. The festivals represent changes in the cycle of the year and can be found in some form among most cultures.

For the Finns, the year was divided into four quarters as noted by four great festivals: Plough Day about April 14, Bear's Day about July 13, Withering Day about October 14, and Collection Day about January 14. Each of these days would be celebrated with appropriate rituals to mark the passage to a new season and to invite the blessings of gods and spirits in the new season's activities. Due to the individualness of Finnish religion, as well as the influence of other cultures, there was a great variety in the observance of times and festivals. As the influence of the Christian religion increased, it was common for the Finnic people to adapt their practices to the Christian calendar. All Saint's Day, for example, was adopted as a continuation of the ancient traditions of honoring the dead. On November 2, it became the practice to prepare a special meal for the dead that could be remembered by name by the head of the family.

Another example of the Finn's syncretic adoption is St. Anthony's Day on January 17. Although nominally a saint's feast day, it was the continuation of the ancient house spirit cult. A rag doll or candle would be prepared to represent the house or farm spirit. This would be kept in a special place, such as the storehouse or grain bin. Later during the year, the doll would be offered food and prayers. These typically coincided with the beginning of the grazing season in spring and again around winter solstice. The farm spirit would also be honored at the time of blizzards with two to three day feasts and offerings of meat, fur, and blood.

Among other important Finnish festivals was the *kesäjuhlat* or summer festival which was celebrated at midsummer (about June 23–24) as Juhannas or St. John's Eve. Midsummer's Day is the longest day of the year. It embodies the love of nature and an appreciation of the forests, flowers, lakes, and rivers. It is a celebration of individuality and creativity.

The festival would begin about June 21 with St. John's Eve. In preparation, the house would be thoroughly cleaned, then decorated by placing arbors of birch trees outside the door and flowers inside the house. This was a time for meditation and the *kokko* or bonfire. It then continued on to June 24, or St. John's Day (the old Midsummer), with a variety of community activities. Anciently, this would include feasts, carousing, and orgies. There would also be leaping and dancing and the sacrifice of wax figurines. Animals would be herded around the fires and fed St. John's flowers and grass to make them fertile and clean. The mistress of the house and other family members, including children, would walk around the fire three times and offer food to the Earth Mother by secretly placing it on a sacrificial stone. Although these are the traditional dates, it was not uncommon to find many smaller celebrations both before and after the formal midsummer's festival.

The *kesäjuhlat,* or summer festival, itself involved athletic contests, singing, dancing, and drama. Typical contests were foot races, broad jumps, high jumps, pole vault, and similar track and field events. A favorite climbing race consisted of climbing the *Juhannus kuusi,* which was a tall slim spruce stripped of bark and branches and placed in the yard. There were also musicians performing both traditional and more contemporary music as solos or in choruses. There were poetry recitations, speeches, dramatic performances, and dancing. And, of course, everyone would sauna.

The Midwinter festival, or Yuletide as it is known in some countries, is the celebration of the Winter Solstice and marks the rebirth of light. It is celebrated around December 21 to 23. This Winter Solstice festival has largely been replaced by the Christmas tradition, but many pagan traditions have continued such as the giving of gifts, the Christmas tree, kissing under the mistletoe, and Santa Claus. The Midwinter festival is a time for joyous celebration and camaraderie. While the Midsummer festival is a celebration of the individual, Midwinter celebrates community and harmony between individuals. It is a time of reunion and togetherness, of rejoicing in rebirth and renewal. It is an appropriate time for resolution and merriment. Particularly important to the Winter Solstice festival is the bonfire or burning of the

Yule log. This is not only a way of calling back the sun, but also of remembering the divine gift of fire, light, and warmth—both as natural and spiritual phenomena. Wishes and concerns for the new year can be inscribed on paper and burnt with the log or bonfire.

The National Winter Festival, or Laskiainen, is celebrated seven weeks before Easter on a Sunday—usually falling around February 7. Old Laskiainen would not begin until the Tuesday after that Sunday in early February, then would continue as days of fasting until Easter. This festival honored women and the handiwork of women. Marking the beginning of the weaving for the year, it was considered bad luck if the spinning was not done by this date. Laskiainen and other winter festivals were also particularly noted as times for the sauna.

The next two important festivals are celebrated at the spring and fall equinoxes. On the equinoxes, the day and night are of equal length. The Spring Equinox occurs between March 21 and 24, marking the first day of spring. It is a celebration of the end of the winter and the arrival of spring. It was celebrated anciently by many cultures, including the Finns, as marking the coming forth of new life. It was known by some of the ancient pre-Christians as Ostara (a term that now lives on in the modern holiday of Easter) and is celebrated with outdoor activities, feasts, and music. The Spring Equinox was particularly associated with cattle breeding as the day for freeing the animals from the barn for the first time in the year, thus marking the beginning of summer and outdoor grazing.

The Autumn Equinox celebrates the first of autumn on about September 21–23. It is a celebration of harvest and thanksgiving, celebrated with feasts, sacrifices, story telling, music, and the sauna.

At the time of the harvest, the first or last sheaf cut would be saved as a symbol of special power. On Christmas Eve, the first sheaf would be brought to the table and offered beer and Christmas food so that the grain would grow well the next year. Then it would be carefully preserved until the next special occasion.

August Eve or August first is the festival of first fruits which is called Lammas in other cultures. It is celebrated with feasting and games.

November Eve (October 31) marks the feast of remembrance. This is the feast known as Samhain by others and which has been diluted into the holiday known as Halloween in modern America. During this time, the ancient shamans believed that the doorway between the seen or material and unseen or immaterial spiritual worlds was open. It is celebrated with sacrifices and ancestral remembrances.

The Finns adapted All Saints' Day as a holy day of remembering and honoring ancestors, but it was also the custom to honor the dead on the Night of New Year's. After the family was asleep, the father would open all the windows and doors and offer the spirits a loaf of bread together with petitions and thanks. When ancestral spirits visited they would be invited to the sauna, then to the family table.

Festivals were also held to honor specific deities or to remember special occasions in clan or family history. These were often family-oriented or individualistic. At other times, they might involve a more complex system of worship. The worship of Pellonpekko, celebrated between Christmas and late March, was a village matter but also involved Peko-fraternities. Pellonpekko was known as "wild one" or "one from the forest," but also "earth king" and "home god." Worshippers would prepare a doll from straw, wood, or wax and give it hair and beard made from flax. It would be given an exaggerated sex organ—and it was common for the figure to change gender from year to year. This doll would then be paraded through the fields to promote fertility.

For the rest of the year, the Peko-worshippers would keep the Peko figure safe. They would offer prayers to Pellonpekko to ask for good crops, household well-being, marital happiness, and protection from hail, frost, and wind. They also participated in secret rituals reminiscent of the mystery cults such as those of Odin, Pythagoras, or the Gnostics.

The position of Peko-priest or Peko-master rotated among worshippers. This person was charged with keeping the Peko figure in his grain bin to bring everything good to the village or to the brotherhood of worshippers. The Peko-priest was chosen through a ritual combat in which the first to have blood drawn was chosen as the Master of the Peko Festival or Peko-priest. In later times, this was a ritualized sham battle. Before the contest, participants ate alone in quiet surrounds, but afterwards they enjoyed a convivial common meal.

The exact nature of the events is not as critical as the celebratory atmosphere of the festival. The festival itself does not have to follow any rigid structure and could just as easily take the form of Scottish games, a Renaissance faire, or even a Fourth of July picnic or similar celebration. The Finns were and are open to a variety of experiences and cultures—a somewhat incongruous example of their eclectic approach to fun is the popularity of the tango in modern Finland—yet perhaps nothing could be more traditionally Finnish than to see Finns dancing the tango in the ancient forests.

Personal Times

Every magus needs to structure personal sacred times. There are some traditions that mandate a series of daily rituals at specific times. The Finnish tradition is more fluid and personal. The mage must find a personal rhythm for the day.

The nature of these personal times will also vary according to the needs and goals of the individual. Most of the time it will involve meditation. This can be enhanced by the sauna, reading, chanting, song, or dance. Personal sacred times can also be special dates such as anniversaries of birth dates and marriages or days of remembrance for ancestors. Traditionally among most Finnic people, Thursday was also given special reverence as a holy day.

Structuring Festivals

Festivals are community and family affairs. Their organization is primarily a matter of logistics. The best way to approach their planning is to begin with the end result in mind, then work backward from the end to determine what must be done—and in what order—to accomplish the desired result.

For example, if the end result is a foot race, then you might envision the end result as an awards ceremony. To have an awards ceremony, there must be awards. There must be some way of judging the contest, so judges or referees will need to be appointed and organized. A race route must be decided and delineated. To have a successful race, there may also be concerns about safety. For example, a long distance race may require watering spots and emergency plans. There must be a way for starting the race. And, to have a race, there must be participants, so there must be a way provided to enter the race—and even before that to advertise or announce the event. By working backward, you can ensure that all details are provided for.

This might at first seem to have little to do with magic, but in fact it is the very essence. The mage visualizes an end result and then, through whatever means are available, causes that end result to take form in the material world. That is magic.

Regardless of the specific agenda involved, a festival should be arranged to encourage celebration. There should be food, song, games, and entertainment. The schedule should be fluid enough to allow for spontaneous diversions, individual choice, and rest. A festival is not an agenda to be filled; it is an opportunity.

Some General Principles for Successful Festivals
1. Choose a significant time and date.
2. Choose a significant location with adequate space.
3. Plan backward from the end.
4. Share the planning with others.
5. Stay flexible.
6. Invoke the spirits for assistance.
7. Give thanks to the spirits for success.

Ancestral Memorials

The haltija of ancestors are important sources of power and wisdom. Although they have passed beyond this reality, they continue to be interested in their families. They watch, and at times intervene, in the affairs of their descendants. Of course, not all ancestral spirits are equal. They vary in power and personality. Some gained such great power that they achieved the status of gods. Others are fairly equal to their mortal counterparts. Some have great wisdom. Others are foolish. Some are benevolent, others are manipulative.

All ancestral spirits gain power through attention. Without the attention of earthly spirits, they tend to lose touch with earth life and lapse into a deep, detached sleep. The attention of mortals gives them focus and motivation.

Mortals, too, gain from the ancestors. We tend to progress through relationships. In marriage, parenthood, and even friendship, we develop virtues and character. We learn to give of ourselves. And through interdependence, we gain strength that would not be attainable to a person working alone. Many are greater than one. Family is mightier than an individual.

The first step in honoring our ancestors is to learn about them. For the ancients, this meant learning the stories—the oral tradition. For moderns it means searching out our roots—the practice of genealogy. Genealogy is one of the most popular hobbies in the world. Many people feel a desire to find out who they are by exploring the history of their family. Undoubtedly some of the interest is prompted by the spirits themselves.

This act of searching out our ancestors is itself an act of devotion that provides surprising benefits. In addition to providing insights into our own identity, it helps us to put into perspective the myths and history of large groups of people. The Kalevala takes on a new meaning when we consider the main figures as ancestors. Similarly, the American Revolutionary War or the American Gold Rush become very real when we learn that family members participated.

Another surprising benefit of discovering our family history is that it increases tolerance. Those who study genealogy soon begin to realize that we are all very literally one family. It appears that all people of European ancestry living today descend from a relatively small percentage of those who lived in the tenth century. This becomes more understandable when you consider all those who died in plagues and wars or for other reasons died childless. In fact, the probability of a person with English ancestry having connections to the British royal house are virtually 100 percent. Moreover, those connections are usually through either Edward I or Edward III—and that includes the current queen as well as many American presidents and ordinary citizens. These are also descendants of Charlemagne, the Magyar princess, Yaroslav of Kiev, Mohammed the Prophet, the chieftains of the Mashwash Libyans, and ancient Egyptian pharaohs! Those are only some of the documented family lines—we really are one family and hence have little basis for intolerance or discrimination.

It is important to learn all that we can about our ancestors, including information important for identification—such as names and dates—but should also include biographical details and stories.

The next step is to record the story. This ensures remembrance and makes the recitation of the story easier. If possible, gather pictures or artifacts that would give some sense of the physical reality of the ancestor.

Recall the story on appropriate occasions. This can be as simple as recalling the names or as complex as a dramatic presentation.

Celebrate the ancestor. This is the process that has been misunderstood by the Christian West as ancestor worship. It is rather the celebration and respect of the ancestor. This is easily done as a memorial meal. The feast can be held in honor of a specific ancestor or of all your ancestors in general. The ancestor or ancestors are remembered and invoked. The meal is offered to them and a token amount of drink and food is offered to the ground and then the meal is eaten by the family. This should be done with a cheerful spirit. Songs, jokes and dancing are more than appropriate.

Honoring Ancestors

1. Learn who your ancestors are. This may take some research.

2. Go to their gravesites, an old homestead, or other significant site or create a shrine with pictures and artifacts. Some ancient Finns would make images or dolls.

3. Invoke the spirits of your ancestors. Invite them to join you and ask for any special request you might have.

4. Celebrate the ancestor by telling stories.

5. Offer the ancestor the memorial meal. Give a small amount of drink and food to the ground.

6. Enjoy the family meal together—the living with the dead. Tell the family stories. Sing, laugh, and dance.

7. Remember to thank the ancestral spirits for their gifts—including your life and heritage.

Personal Times

1. Choose the time that feels best to you. This should be the same time every day and a special time once a week at a minimum.
2. Use the same place every time, if possible. It should be comfortable and quiet.
3. Arrange your schedule so that others will not be able to infringe on that time.
4. Prepare yourself mentally and physically. If a sauna ritual is not possible, then at least wash your face and hands and relax.
5. Invoke the spirits of the place and time.
6. The best use of this solitude is in quiet meditation. Other useful practices would include drumming and singing of sacred songs. Reading, studying, planning, and other "left-brained" activities should be avoided.
7. When the time is up, take a few deep breaths and thank the spirits.

Dancing

Magical dancing is a fundamental tool of the Finnish mage. It combines characteristics of ritual and music. In addition to enhancing physical health and improving one's ability to deal with stress, dancing can be done as a form of meditation. It can be done as a means of conducting a shamanic journey to gain knowledge and power. Through the dance, the mage can enter an alternate reality where the haltija of animals, ancestors, gods, or others will guide and instruct. The dance can also be done to effect some change in the world—the ancients used dance to ensure successful hunting and harvests. But despite the variety of uses, the elements of the dance are simple.

The basic elements of the magical dance are sound and movement. For those who understand, any dance (or any action for that matter) is an act of magic. Once that is understood, then any magic or dance form can be used.

The traditional method involved drums or rattles. The modern practitioner can use a drum, but a tape can be used as well. The mage can also dance to singing or to the music of other instruments such as the kantele. A very workable alternative or adjunct is to carry or wear a rattle. As with any magical practice, the choice of instrument should be a matter of personal preference based on what works best rather than on tradition.

The Basic Dance

Regardless of what musical instrument is chosen, the music should have a constant steady beat. It should start relatively slowly and then gradually increase as the mage enters trance and begins the journey. It also helps to dance in a setting that is semi-dark and in which you will not be disturbed.

The dance should begin as a simple up and down motion. Concentrate on the sound. Allow yourself to mentally travel to a place you enjoy and find peaceful and relaxing. That will be the place to begin each journey. It could be the seashore, or the forest, or any other setting where you feel safe and comfortable. Dance there for at least five minutes, just allowing yourself to move to the beat. Immerse yourself physically in the sound while you mentally become involved in the journey.

The Journey

After you have danced the basic dance for at least five minutes, you can begin the journey. Follow the images. At some point, you will meet a guide. Listen to the guide. Follow where the guide leads.

To dance a journey is to act out what you can see and hear. For example, if you see animals, imitate them in your dance. Dance the terrain and your movements through the terrain. If your journey involves flight or descent, then you may find that a ladder or stairs help you to find your destination more easily.

On the journey you will be able to gain magical tools. Pick them up and bring them back. They will become resources to you in future journeys.

Pay attention to what you see and hear on your journey. This is how you learn words of knowledge and power. In particular, you can gain new songs while on your journey. Dance the new songs and remember them for future use.

When you have gained your tools or power words, return the way you came. You will often find that the return is very quick. Allow the sound to pull you back.

Dancing Magic

You can also dance changes in the world through the dance. The dance will help focus your power and attention. To use this, begin with the basic dance for several minutes.

As you dance, focus on the process you would like to see occur. The archetype of this sort of dance is the hunting dance of the ancients. During the dance they dance their travel, the search for game, stalking the prey, the animal itself, the kill, and the successful return. The dancer or dancers would focus their attention and emotions in the process. For the modern mage, the goal might be different, but the method essentially the same. Dance the story that you want to see happen. Dance as much detail of the story as possible, with as much passion as possible.

Other Dances

Though not strictly considered dancing, there are other movements that the mage uses to increase in power. Any rhythmic movement can be used to facilitate trance. Such activities are sometimes known as "moving meditation" and can include chopping wood, swimming, walking, and running.

Summary

Mastering the three principles presented in this chapter can enhance your magical workings. The key is the Basic Dance technique, which can be modified and incorporated into a number of magical workings, including The Journey and Dancing Magic.

The Basic Dance

1. Begin with a steady simple up and down motion.
2. Concentrate on the sound.
3. Let your mind travel to a safe comfortable place.
4. Dance for at least five minutes.

The Journey

1. Begin with the basic dance.
2. Follow the images and your guide.
3. Dance the journey by dancing what you see and hear. Dance your movements through the terrain.
4. Pay attention and bring back any tools, power words, or new songs.
5. Return quickly with what you have gained.

Dancing Magic

1. Begin with the basic dance.
2. Focus on the process you would like to see occur.
3. Dance the story you want to happen.
4. Dance a successful return.

The Symbols of Magic

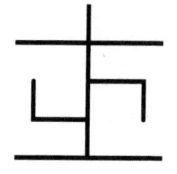

There is no set of orthodox or required symbols that must be used in Finnish magic. There are, of course, several traditional symbols that have gained cultural significance over the ages. The modern mage should not feel obligated or limited by those symbols however.

There are several general principles that seem to apply to the use of symbols in Finnish magic. The first is that natural symbols are preferred over artificial symbols.

There seems to be more magic in a stone, piece of wood, fossil, shell, claw from a bird or animal, or similar object than in a manufactured icon or talisman. That is not to say, however, that the manufactured symbol is not used—the Sampo itself was a product of technology. But generally, the mage prefers objects that are discovered in nature. These items might be found while in trance, or they could be serendipitous finds that the mage feels drawn to.

A symbol is more effective when it is made by the person who is to use it. That person will know best their purpose and will invest the symbol with will through invocations, petitions, and rituals. He or she will know best how to shape it and with what colors and textures it should be given character.

The best symbols are simple. There is no requirement for intricate workmanship or expert craftsmanship. Of course, the true mage will put only the best effort into such work, but it need not be supposed that every mage must be an artist or craftsman; it is helpful if they are, but this dexterity is not a requirement. Even in cases when the mage has great artistic skill, the stylistic preference in Finnish magical symbolism is for simple line drawings and abstract representations.

Of course, these principles are not binding upon the mage. Each mage must choose the symbols that do the most to increase focus, thus increasing power.

Ancient Finnish Symbols

Traditional Finnish symbols frequently include the images of gods; these are often found on the drums of shamans. As can be seen by the picture of Ukko and Akko, below, these are usually simply very abstract line drawings.

Top: Ukko; Bottom: Akko

Another frequent drawing found on drums is that of the shaman. This most often represents the shaman with a drum, as shown below. Other drawings might include animals or activities such as the hunt, voyaging, or the harvest. It would also be appropriate to draw pictures of the shaman in flight or other magical activities.

A Shaman Drawing

Abstract symbols can also be used. The *hannunvarkuna*—which is now seen as a common decorative motif in Finland, Karelia, and Estonia—was originally placed as a protective sign on buildings or on objects. As seen below, it consists of a concentric square with externally looped corners.

The hannunvarkuna

Many of the commonly used symbols were borrowed from the Norse. The Hammer of Thor was used on drums and to decorate altars. The Sun Wheel, which is also sometimes called the Hammer of Thor, represents the eternal cycle. It was used as a charm to gain the protection of Thor. Also known as the swastika, this widespread symbol has unfortunately been tainted by evil men in this century.

Talismans and Amulets

Talismans used to attract good luck and amulets used to dispel bad luck are common in Finnish magic. Again, natural objects are preferred. The objects were usually kept in a leather pouch, which would often include herbs. These symbols were usually line drawings like the hannunvarkuna and could be worn or placed on objects. Following are several examples.

to ward off the negative and protect from enemies

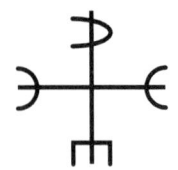

to prevent others from planting an evil spell

love charm

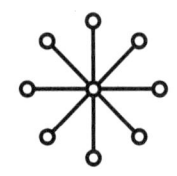

drawn on paper or birch wood and placed under the pillow to make dreams come true

to heal sickness

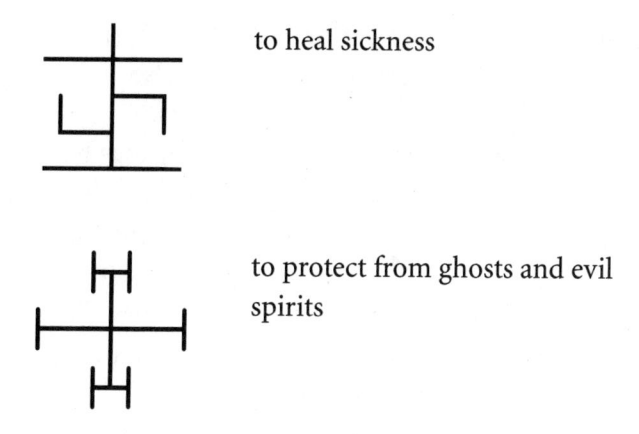

to protect from ghosts and evil spirits

Runes

Runes, or futhark, were closely associated with magic. The word *rune* itself was adopted to describe the songs of magic found in the Kalevala. The word is related to the Indo-European *Ru* meaning secret or mystery and the Old High German *runar,* meaning whisper. "Whispering mystery" well describes the attitude of the ancients toward this knowledge.

Although closely associated with the Nordic people, there are several runic alphabets with widespread use among Finnic people and their relatives. Runes have been found throughout northern Eurasia. Runic monuments have been found around the upper course of the Yenisei in eastern Siberia, in the Valley of Oakhorn in the Mongolian People's Republic, and in the area east of the Oakhorn, including an area not far from Ulan Bator. One of the largest runic monuments was discovered near the Selenga River in Siberia by Gustaf John Ramstedt, a

Finnish linguist and founder of Mongolian linguistics and Altaic comparative studies. Runes were also used to write books of divination by the Manichaeans.

Their origin is shrouded in mystery. They may have originated with Etruscan alphabet and been introduced to the Baltic region by traders seeking amber. But that is only speculation. Throughout Eurasia they were treated as sacred and connected with divine mysteries. They were widely used by the northern Germanic people, including the Scandinavians and the English. Some might object to their use in Finnish magic though, as we have already seen, they were by no means exclusively Germanic. Additionally, it should be kept in mind that the old Finns borrowed and adapted from their neighbors—there was a blending of people and cultures. It is not surprising then to find that runes were used in calendars much later in Estonia and Finland than in Sweden. There is a runic monument at Hiiumaa, in the north, dated 1796.

Runes were especially important in the cult of Odin and were closely associated with that shaman-god. They should not be taken lightly—they do not give up their secrets easily, as evidenced by the story of Odin who hung on Yggdrasill in order to gain those secrets. Before using them, the mage should invoke the spirits for protection.

Runes can be used in a number of ways. A single rune or several runes can be used as a charm and in the making of amulets. They can also be used in healing rituals (especially on Odin's day or Wednesday). They can also be used for divination. They can be used to add power to rituals or ritual objects. The use of runes is beyond the scope of this book but for those who are interested, there are several books available. The many uses of runes can be seen in the following excerpt from a poem that is said to have been written by Odin himself to instruct rune masters.

> *Know'st how to write, know'st how to read,*
> *know'st how to stain, how to understand,*
> *know'st how to ask, know'st how to offer,*
> *know'st how to supplicate, know'st how*
> *   to sacrifice?*
>
> *'Tis better unasked than offered overmuch;*
> *for ay doth a gift look for gain;*
> *'tis better unasked than offered overmuch:*
> *thus did Öthin write ere the earth began,*
> *when up he rose in after time.*
>
> *Those spells I know which the spouses of kings*
> *Wot not, nor earthly wight:*
> *"Help" one is hight, with which holpen thou'lt be*
> *in sorrow and care and sickness.*
>
> *That other I know which all will need*
> *who leeches list to be:*
> *(on the bark scratch them of bole in the woods*
> *whose boughs bend to the east).*[1]

If you wish to incorporate runes into your magic, remember that it is better to make your own. Preferred woods are oak, ash, or yew. Use fallen branches when possible. If you must cut a tree, first ask permission of the tree and leave an offering or libation when you are finished. The shape, size, and color of the runes is a matter of personal choice and intuition. After they are prepared, consecrate them with salt water and keep them in a small pouch with a drawstring when not in use.

Caution should be taken when using the runes. Runes should be treated reverently. Each rune is associated with an elemental spirit or force. Disrespect will only invite the anger of these forces. Even when used reverently, the rune magic (or any magic for that matter) may set in motion a chain of events that the mage might later regret. As Odin said in the poem above: *"'Tis better unasked than offered overmuch; for ay doth a gift look for gain."*

When using the runes, it is important to remember that it took the ancient rune masters many years to learn the inner meanings of runes. That process of learning is not merely a matter of reading books, but of personal discipline—Odin himself hung on Yggdrasill to learn those mysteries.

A healing ritual involving runes begins with quiet meditation and, when possible, a sauna. Invoke the gods. Write the name of the person to be healed. Invoke the gods again, particularly Odin and Baldur, and ask them to heal the person. Write the desired healing together with the person's name. Burn the petition and visualize the healing spreading out from the flame. Give thanks to the gods. A symbolic sacrifice such as burning a hair, a drop of blood or a libation should also be made.

Runes were often used by the ancient Finns to add power to ritual objects. Runes can be inscribed on ritual objects such as drums. Runes can also be used to write out the words of charms and petitions. These can be inscribed on objects such as eating utensils or tools or even doorframes or walls. They can also be written on tree barks then ritually burned to send the petition to the gods.

Runes can be used to make talismans. These might consist of a rune or runes on a piece of paper that is kept in a bag around the neck. They can also consist of more complex talismans such as wooden carvings or metal that is engraved or shaped. Another alternative and a favorite of the ancients was to engrave a ring. Talismans should be constructed in conjunction with the invocation of the gods and shamanic ritual.

When using runes for inscribing objects or making talismans, it is important for the mage to attend closely to the intuitions that indicate the guidance of the spirits. If possible, precede the use of runes with the sauna. Spend time in quiet meditation and seek the guidance of the spirits while you are in trance. The actual runes used depends as much on intuitive insight as it does on some rigid formulaic interpretation of the runes. At times, a single rune or a group of runes is all that is needed. At other times, the mage may write out in detail the words of sacred songs or petitions to the gods.

Runes can also be used for divination. When this is done, it is good to invoke Odin and Freya, the traditional guardians of runic knowledge. Ask for guidance that

```
        ┌───┐
        │ 1 │
        └───┘
┌───┐ ┌───┐ ┌───┐
│ 4 │ │ 5 │ │ 2 │
└───┘ └───┘ └───┘
        ┌───┐
        │ 3 │
        └───┘
```

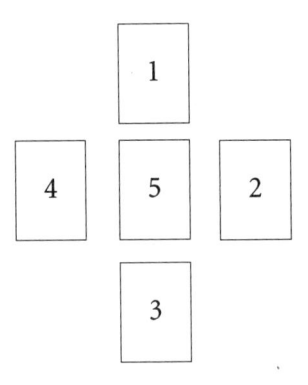

The Cross of Thor

your question might be answered. Formulate a question in your mind. It should be as clear and specific as possible. Avoid "yes and no" questions. The runes are shaken or shuffled and a number of runes are chosen at random. They can also be shaken and cast onto a flat surface covered by a cloth.

The simplest method used for a reading is to choose three runes and place them side by side. There are other methods for longer readings, including the popular Cross of Thor (see diagram above). With this approach, four runes are cast and placed in the center of an equilateral cross. A fifth is then chosen and placed in the center of the cross. Starting at the top, the runes are numbered with the top rune as number one. The center rune is five. One represents general influences in the situation. Two represents obstacles. Three represents favorable forces. Four shows short-term or immediate consequences. And five shows long-term consequences.

Anciently, there were several systems of runes. These varied according to the language of the area; the runes of Britain were different from those of Scandinavia and Germany, for example. The Finns modified the runes for their use according to their culture and intuitive insight. The following list provides a very brief introduction to the runes and their meanings. There are several good books available on runes if you wish to have more information.

Rune	Sound	Name and Meaning
ᚠ	f	**Fee, Feyu** Cattle, wealth. Power that must be circulated. Money, success.
ᚢ	u	**Ur, Urus** Wild ox. Power. Spiritual strength. Individualism. Good fortune. Health.
ᚦ	th	**Thorn, Porn** A thorn. The hammer of Thor. Sometimes translated as demon or giant. Protection. An important decision. Good news. Unexpected luck. Banishing power.

ᚮ, ᚭ   o   **Os, Ose**
Odin. The divine rune. Sacred to Odin. Communication through written and spoken word. Wisdom.

ᚱ   r   **Ride, Rad**
Wheel. Associated with travel.

ᚻ   ch   **Char, Cen**
Associated with sacred fires on hilltops at the solstices and equinoxes. Spiritual enlightenment. Artistic creativity. Discerning power.

ᚷ   g/j   **Gyfu, Gibbet**
Gifts (Gyfu). Gallows (Gibbet). Gifts and sacrifices. Important to relationships. Shared love. Binding together a relationship.

ᚹ   w   **Wyn**
Joy. Sometimes link to Odin.

ᚺ   h   **Hagel**
Hail or Air. Symbolizes unexpected spring storms. Delays and limitations in daily life or spiritual growth.

ᚾ   n   **Nyd**
Need. Can represent Wyrd or destiny. Ruled by the Norns, goddesses of fate. Caution. Power of the present.

ᛁ   i   **Is**
Ice. Opposite to Cen. The second primal rune. End of activity. Formulation of the future.

ᛄ   y   **Ger**
Year. Symbol of growth, rebirth, regeneration and harvest. Wheel or cycle of the seasons. The line represents Midwinter and Midsummer. Sacred to the Norns and to Frey. A warning not to judge. End of a cycle.

ᛇ   y   **Eoh**
Yew. Death. The yew is sacred to Odin. Yggdrasill was said to be a yew tree. Best wood for carving runes. The power of the will. Shaman's rune. Death. News of a friend or enemy. Recurrence of an old problem.

ᛈ   p   **Peorth**
Hearth. Also, fruit tree and chessmen. Connected with games of chance and so with Wyrd. Also linked with sacred music, bardism and the sacred dance. Hidden knowledge. Unexpected gain. Power of space.

ᛉ   x   **Eolh**
Elks. Protection. Used to warn away trespassers. Derives from an ancient hand symbol used to ward off spirits—palm of hand outwards and raised three fingers.

ᛋ   s   **Sigil**
Sun. Health. Wise direction. Life force. Feminine energy.

ᛏ   t   **Tyr, Tiw**
The god Tyr or Tiw. Victory in battle. Divine justice. Male energy in positive form. Emotional fulfillment. Sexual relationship. Success with legal issues.

ᛒ b **Beorc**
Birch. Symbol of fertility.
Birth rune. Lucky rune. Dispels
misfortune. New beginnings.

ᛖ e **Eh, Eean**
Horse. Sacred to Odin and Frey.
Travel. Job changes.

ᛚ l **Lagu**
Lake or sea. Womb of the mother
goddess. Source of life. Awakens
psychic powers. Intuition.

ᛝ ng **Ing**
The god Ing. Symbol of fertility.
Sexual polarity. Union of
opposites. Realization of a dream.

ᛞ d **Daeg**
Day. Dawn of a new day. Symbol
Midsummer. Prosperity.

ᛟ o **Odal**
Home. Property. Legacies.

ᚪ   a   **Ansuz**
Ash. Arcane wisdom through visions. Power of intellect.

ᛇ   y   **Yielding**

ᛠ   ea   **Earth**

ᛡ   eo   **Yeowell**
Wheel of the year.

ᛢ   q(u)   **Quern**
Grain mill.

ᛣ   c/k   **Cup**

ᛥ   st   **Stone**

Endnote
1. Lee M. Hollander, trans. *The Poetic Edda* (Austin, TX: University of Texas Press, 1996) 37–41.

Conclusion

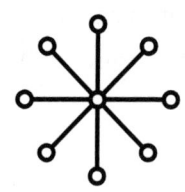

The magic of the Finns is built on the same fundamental principles that can be found in the magic of all people. It is built first on the idea that there are spirits in all things. The mage seeks to understand and to respect these spirits. Magic in a certain sense is a matter of building relationships with the spirits.

It is a matter of character and reverence. The secret of magic is the spiritual development of the mage. Those who would wish to sing the power songs with the authority of the ancient mages must be willing to spend the effort to develop their own character first. That is the meaning of many of the old stories. The secrets of the ancients are not given away easily. They must be pried from the mouth of Antero Vipunen. They require sacrifice and complete devotion. The mage may have to hang from Yggdrasill as did Odin.

The magic of the Finns derives from tradition—that is to say that it derives from the experiences of former mages. But it is more than the experience of mages that comprises the magical tradition. It is the tradition of human experience. It is a matter of families and culture. Each family has important traditions and stories to pass on, as does each culture. It is in these traditions that we can understand our own humanity. It is through that understanding that we can work magic.

Appendix:
Finnish Language

Finnish belongs to a widespread language family known as Ural-Altaic. The name refers to the Altai and Ural mountains where these languages and people are supposed to have originated. This great family has members throughout Asia and includes Korean, Mongol, Turkish, as well as Finnish. More specifically, Finnish belongs to the sub-group known as Finno-Ugric. Speakers of Finno-Ugric include Ugrian (Voguls, Ostyaks in Western Siberia and Magyars), Permian

(Zyrians, Votyaks, and Permians who live in Vyatka and Perm Provinces in Russia), Cheremis-Mordvin (Cheremis on the left bank of the Upper Volga and Mordvins on the Middle Volga), and the Western Group which includes the Finns, Karelians, Estonians, Livonians, and Lapps.

In pronouncing Finnish words the stress is always on the first syllable. Intonation is fairly even—questions and statements have the same intonation. That is, there is no rising tone at the end of a question. The following information should provide the reader with enough information to pronounce the various names and terms mentioned in the text.

There are thirteen consonants which are similar in pronunciation to English consonants. Double consonants are three times longer than single consonants.

Vowels are pronounced as follows:

/a/ is like the u in run. Example: Jumala.
/aa/ is like the a in father.
/ä/ is like the a in hat.
/ö/ is like the e in never.
/y/ is like the ui in suit.

Other vowels are pronounced as in Spanish or Japanese Romaji.

Dipthongs give full value to each value. The /äi/ in Väinämöinen is pronounced as the ay in say in Australian English. The /öi/ is like the vowel sound of bird when said in a Bronx dialect.

Bibliography

———. *Transcript of the Trial of Margaret Matson.* Colonial Records of Pennsylvania 1:95.

Castaneda, Carlos. *The Teachings of Don Juan: A Yaqui Way of Knowledge.* Berkeley and Los Angeles, CA: University of California Press, 1968.

Coffin, T.P. and Cohen, H. *Folklore in America.* Garden City, New York: Doubleday and Co., 1996.

Cunningham, S. *Magical Herbalism.* St. Paul, MN: Llewellyn, 1982.

Dana, Richard Henry. *Two Years Before the Mast.* New York: Collier and Son, 1909.

Eliade, Mircea. *Shamanism: Archaic Techniques of Ecstasy.* New York: Pantheon, 1964.

Frazer, James George. *The Golden Bough*. New York: Collier Books, 1922.

Friberg, Eino, trans. *The Kalevala: Epic of the Finnish People*. Helsinki, Finland: Otava Publishing Company Ltd., 1988.

Gurdjieff. *Meeting with Remarkable Men*. New York: E. P. Dutton, 1991.

Harner, Michael. *The Way of the Shaman: A Guide to Power and Healing*. New York: Bantam, 1980.

Hollander, Lee M., trans. *The Poetic Edda*. Austin, TX: University of Texas Press, 1996.

Howard, Michael. *Understanding Runes*. Glasgow, Scotland: The Aquarian Press, 1990.

Kirby, W. F., trans. *Kalevala: The Land of the Heroes*. London and Dover, NH: The Athlone Press, 1985.

Louhi, E.A. *The Delaware Finns or the First Permanent Settlements in Pennsylvania, Delaware, West New Jersey and Eastern Part of Maryland*. Humanity Press: New York, 1925.

Mason, Bernard S. *How to Make Drums, Tomtoms, and Rattles: Primitive Percussion Instruments for Modern Use*. New York: Dover, 1974.

Matthews, John. *The Druid Source Book from Earliest Times to the Present Day*. London: Blandford Press, 1996.

Murray, Margaret A. *The Witch-Cult in Western Europe*. Oxford: Oxford University Press, 1967.

Nelson, R. E. *Nelson Family History*. Privately published, 1992.

Nelson, Robert. *A Pennsylvania Witch*. The Augustan Society Omnibus. Book 14, 1993.

Olin, S.C. *Finlandia The Racial Composition, The Language and a Brief History of the Finnish People*. Hancock, MI: The Book Concern, 1957.

Rajanen, Aini. *Of Finnish Ways*. Minneapolis, MN: Dillon Press, 1981.

Starhawk. *The Spiral Dance*. New York: Harper and Row, 1979.

Van Name, Elmer G. *Anthony Nelson Seventeenth Century Pennsylvania and New Jersey and Some of his Descendants*. Haddonfield, NJ, 1962.

Weslager, C. A. *The Log Cabin in America: From Pioneer Day to the Present*. New Brunswick, NJ: Rutgers University Press, 1969.

Index

A

Aestii, 2
Ahto, Ahti, 56
Akko, 50, 141
alchemy, 37
ancestors, 2, 17, 48, 59–60, 101, 124, 126, 128–131, 133
ancestral memorials, 128–131
Ascomanni, 4
Aske, 50

B

Baldur, 52, 54–55, 148
Balto-Finns, 2
baptism, 18
bards, 28–29, 31, 37, 41, 104
basic dance, 134–137
basic trance, 68–69
Beormas, 4
berserkers, 52
Bishop Henry of Uppsala, 4, 18

C

Campbell, J. F., 3
celestial gods, 49–50
chants, chanting, 15–17, 31, 48, 63, 67, 72, 84, 94, 98, 101, 126
charms, 12, 28–29, 31–32, 47, 57–58, 90, 101, 103, 106–109, 143–144, 146, 149
Chester, Pennsylvania, 11–12
children of Kalevala, 2
Christianity, 18, 22
Cosmic Tree, 38
Cross of Thor, 150

D

Dame of the North Farm, 41
Dana, Richard Henry, 13, 24
dancing magic, 136–137
Delaware, 6–7, 9–10, 12, 19
Delaware Valley, 6–7, 9–10, 19
doppelganger, 47
dreams, 59–60, 71, 144, 154
drums, 13, 15, 37, 53, 68, 75, 79, 97–98, 117, 134, 141–143, 149

E

eagles, 38–39, 79, 89
earth divinities, 55–58
Egyptian mythology, 33
equinox, 119, 123–124
Estonia, 2, 143, 146
Euhemerus, 41

F

festivals, 120–126
festival structure, 120–126
finngerd, 3
Finno-Ugrians, 3
fly agaric mushroom, 23, 72
Fort Ross, California, 6
Frazer, James George, 13, 24
Frey, 13, 54, 74, 153–154
Freya, 54, 74, 149
Frigg, Frigga, 54–55

G

goddess worship, 57
Great Candle Movement, 18

guardian angels, 60
Gurdjieff, 41

H

Hakkapelis, 4
haltija, 43–48, 50, 59–61, 77–78, 114, 128, 133
Hammer of Thor, 53, 143, 151
hannunvarkuna, 143–144
Hanson, John, 11
healing, 2, 10, 16, 77, 79, 96, 105–106, 111, 113, 115, 146, 148
Hel, 54
Hermes, 52
Hiisi, 34, 58, 79
Holy Grail, 39
house father, 57
huuhta, 8

I

Ilma, 50
Ilmarinen, 16, 23, 31, 33–37, 98, 104
Ilmater, 32, 40
Ingimud the Old, 13
Isanen, 50

J

Joukahainen, 33, 42
Jumala, 17, 49–50, 105
juurigen, 8

K

Kaleva, 17, 26, 32, 41–42
Kalevala, 2–3, 5, 12, 15–18, 21, 23–42, 50, 57–58, 64–67, 79, 89, 92, 94–95, 100, 104, 108, 110, 129, 145
kantele, 10, 22, 32, 39, 105, 134
Kanteletar, 29
Karelia, 21, 28, 34, 143
kaski, 8
King Eric the Good, 4
kirja, 81, 91
Kugu Sorta, 18
Kullervo, 34–36, 57
Kuu, 50
Kuutar, 50

L

Lalli, 18
Lapps, 2–4, 13–14, 18, 23, 41–42, 51, 53, 79
Laskiainen, 123

learning from nature, 78–79, 84, 86, 91
Leif Erickson, 6
Lemminkäinen, 31, 34, 56, 58
Lempi, 34
Lenni Lenape, 11
log cabins, 9–10
Loki, 54–55, 79
Lönnrot, Elias, 28–29, 31–32, 37
loyly, 46–47, 50, 115–116
Luonnotar, 50

M

Magnus, Albertus, 16
Manala, 58
Mano, 50
Matson, Margaret, 11, 19–20, 56
Matson, Nils, 11, 19–20, 56
Mehilainen, 55
mermaids, 19, 56
Midsummer, 64, 119, 121–122, 153–154
Midwinter, 122, 153
Mielikki, 56
Mimir, 51
Mjollnir, 53, 55
Morton, John, 11
Mortonson, Morton, 11
Mother of Metsula, 55
music, 63, 67, 93–96, 98–100, 104, 122–124, 133–134, 153

N

Nakki, 47, 87
national winter festival, 123
Native Americans, 6, 72, 114
nature, 15–16, 30, 36, 46, 48–49, 52, 54–55, 67, 77–92, 94, 100–103, 120–121, 126, 140
nature spirits, 55–58
Nelson, Anthony, 10, 21, 24
New Jersey, 6–7, 9, 21, 24
New Sweden, 6, 19–20, 112
Norse gods, 50–55
Nothnagle Cabin, 9, 21
Nyyrikki, 56

O

Odin, 39, 50–54, 60, 74, 125, 146–149, 151–154, 158
Odinic Mysteries, 52–54

Ohthera, 4
oral tradition, 2, 27–28, 31, 40–41, 129
Orn, 19, 56
Otava, 50

P

Paakkunainen, Seppo, 95
Paha, 57–58
Paiva, 50
Paivatar, 50
Peko-master, 125
Peko-priest, 125
Pellervoinen, 55, 89
Pellonpekko, 125
Penn, William, 20
Pennsylvania, 6–7, 11–12, 20, 24
Pieve, 50
pirti, 8–9
power songs, 84, 158
protective spirits, 60

R

Raud, 19
Rauni, 50
ritual, 29–30, 33, 37, 51–53, 63–64, 66–75, 88, 96, 125, 132–133, 147–149
ritual preparation, 64–65

Roosevelt, Franklin D., 11
runes, 29, 51–52, 54, 66, 81, 145–151, 153
runo, runoi, 29, 32–33, 40

S

sacred places, 61, 86–89
sacred rivers, sacred lakes, 86
sacred times, 119–132
sacrifice, 61, 73–75, 83, 121, 147–148, 158
Saga of Olaf Tryggvason, 18
Saint Nicholas, 22
sampo, 16, 22, 25, 34, 36–39, 140
Santa Claus, 22–23, 122
sauna, 10, 15, 23, 50, 57, 66, 70, 72, 111–117, 122–124, 126, 132, 148–149
Savo-Karelian Finns, 7
sejda (sacred stone), 68, 88
shadow spirit, 46
shaman songs, 95, 100
shamans, shamanism, 2, 10, 13–15, 17, 21, 23, 25–26, 32–33, 37–39, 41–42, 51, 53–54, 58,

70, 72, 79, 84, 94–100, 117, 124, 133, 141–142, 146, 149, 153
shaman songs, 95–97
shapeshifting, 54, 69–70, 73
Sibelius, Jean, 40, 95
Siberia, 53, 95, 145
sisu (will), 4–5, 64
Sitka, Alaska, 6
solstice, 119, 121–122
songs, singing, 10, 14–16, 19, 22–23, 26–29, 31–34, 37, 39–40, 56, 63, 66–67, 70, 78, 80, 84–85, 88, 93–110, 117, 122, 126–127, 131–132, 134–135, 137, 145, 149, 158
spirits, 2, 14–17, 37–38, 43–62, 66–67, 69, 73, 78–79, 85–88, 90, 96–97, 99, 101–105, 120, 124, 128–129, 131–132, 145–146, 149, 153, 157
St. George's Night, 18
summer festival, 121–122
Suonetar, 55
Swedesboro, 7, 9–10

T

Tacitus, 2–3
talismans, 47, 88, 140, 144, 149
Tapio, 16–17, 55, 78
Thor, 50, 53, 55, 74, 143, 150–151
Thorfinn, 6
Thoth, 52
totems, 38, 48, 54, 99
Tuonela, 17, 34, 36, 58, 95
Tuonetar, 59
Tuoni, 16, 58–59, 101
Tursas, 56
Tuulikki, 56

U

Ukko (also Jumala), 17, 49–50, 61, 79, 141
Ukko Ylijumala, 50, 61
Underworld, 25, 49, 58–59, 96, 98–99
Untamoinen, 34–35
Uppsala, 4, 18, 51
Ursa Major, 38
Ursa Minor, 38

V

Väinämöinen, 3, 5, 15–17, 21–23, 31–33, 38,

41–42, 50, 58, 60, 79, 89, 97, 101, 104, 117
Veden Haltia, 56
Vellamo, 56
Vetehinen, 56
Vipunen, Antero, 17, 41, 101, 158
visions, 26, 37, 71–72, 84–85, 114, 155
Volga-Finns, 2

W

wind, 13–14, 46, 51, 59, 107, 109, 125
wind magic, 13
water divinities, 55–58
World Tree, 38, 49, 51, 88

Y

Yggdrasill, 39, 51, 74, 146, 148, 153

☾ REACH FOR THE MOON

Llewellyn publishes hundreds of books on your favorite subjects! To get these exciting books, including the ones on the following pages, check your local bookstore or order them directly from Llewellyn.

ORDER BY PHONE
- Call toll-free within the U.S. and Canada, 1-800-THE MOON
- In Minnesota, call (612) 291-1970
- We accept VISA, MasterCard, and American Express

ORDER BY MAIL
- Send the full price of your order (MN residents add 7% sales tax) in U.S. funds, plus postage & handling to:

    Llewellyn Worldwide
    P.O. Box 64383, Dept. K489-8
    St. Paul, MN 55164–0383, U.S.A.

POSTAGE & HANDLING
(For the U.S., Canada, and Mexico)
- $4.00 for orders $15.00 and under
- $5.00 for orders over $15.00
- No charge for orders over $100.00

We ship UPS in the continental United States. We ship standard mail to P.O. boxes. Orders shipped to Alaska, Hawaii, The Virgin Islands, and Puerto Rico are sent first-class mail. Orders shipped to Canada and Mexico are sent surface mail.

International orders: Airmail—add freight equal to price of each book to the total price of order, plus $5.00 for each non-book item (audio tapes, etc.).

Surface mail—Add $1.00 per item.

Allow 2 weeks for delivery on all orders.
Postage and handling rates subject to change.

DISCOUNTS
We offer a 20% discount to group leaders or agents. You must order a minimum of 5 copies of the same book to get our special quantity price.

FREE CATALOG
Get a free copy of our color catalog, *New Worlds of Mind and Spirit*. Subscribe for just $10.00 in the United States and Canada ($30.00 overseas, airmail). Many bookstores carry *New Worlds*—ask for it!

Visit our web site at www.llewellyn.com for more information.

Celtic Magic

D. J. Conway

Many people, not all of Irish descent, have a great interest in the ancient Celts and the Celtic pantheon, and *Celtic Magic* is the map they need for exploring this ancient and fascinating magical culture.

Celtic Magic is for the reader who is either a beginner or intermediate in the field of magic. It provides an extensive "how-to" of practical spell-working. There are many books on the market dealing with the Celts and their beliefs, but none guide the reader to a practical application of magical knowledge for use in everyday life. There is also an in-depth discussion of Celtic deities and the Celtic way of life and worship, so that an intermediate practitioner can expand upon the spellwork to build a series of magical rituals. Presented in an easy-to-understand format, *Celtic Magic* is for anyone searching for new spells that can be worked immediately, without elaborate or rare materials, and with minimal time and preparation.

0-87542-136-9, mass market, 240 pp., illus. $4.99

To order, call 1–800 THE MOON
prices subject to change without notice

Norse Magic

D. J. Conway

The Norse: adventurous Viking wanderers, daring warriors, worshippers of the Aesir and the Vanir. Like the Celtic tribes, the Northmen had strong ties with the Earth and Elements, the Gods and the "little people."

Norse Magic is an active magic, only for participants, not bystanders. It is a magic of pride in oneself and the courage to face whatever comes. It interests those who believe in shaping their own future, those who believe that practicing spellwork is preferable to sitting around passively waiting for changes to come.

The book leads the beginner step by step through the spells. The in-depth discussion of Norse deities and the Norse way of life and worship set the intermediate student on the path to developing his or her own active rituals. *Norse Magic* is a compelling and easy-to-read introduction to the Norse religion and Teutonic mythology. The magical techniques are refreshingly direct and simple, with a strong feminine and goddess orientation.

0-87542-137-7, mass market, 240 pp., illus.   **$4.99**

To order, call 1–800 THE MOON
prices subject to change without notice

Slavic Sorcery
Shamanic Journey of Initiation
Kenneth Johnson

In Eastern Europe and European Russia, the spiritual world of primordial hunters is still alive, even though their hearth-fires are long cold. Until now, few scholars were even aware that a magickal tradition still existed in the land now inhabited by Slavic peoples.

Author Kenneth Johnson presents his true-life experiences with the living practitioners of a magickal discipline extending back into pre-Christian times. Johnson traveled to Russia and studied with several Slavic sorcerers, one of whom took him under his wing and put him through extensive training in Pagan Earth Magic.

Slavic Sorcery serves as a course in authentic shamanic practices. For Pagans or individuals of Slavic descent, this book also serves as an introduction to the mythology and lore of the Slavic peoples, covering the seasonal festivals, cosmology, the gods, the Otherworld spirits, and beliefs about the ancestors.

1-56718-374-3, 6 x 9, 224 pp., softcover   **$12.95**

To order, call 1–800 THE MOON
prices subject to change without notice